WHERE ARE YOU GOING?

A Guide to the Spiritual Journey

SWAMI MUKTANANDA

First Printing: September 1981
Second Printing: January 1982

Edited by Sally Kempton.
Assistant Editors: Mary Nevader with George Franklin.
Cover design by Swami Muktananda; painting by Susan Theresa Smith.
Inside design by Bruce Montgomery.

Printed in the United States of America.
P.O. Box 600, South Fallsburg, New York 12779.
ISBN: 0-914602-72-6 LCCN: 81-52192

CONTENTS

BHAGAWAN NITYANANDA, SWAMI MUKTANANDA'S GURU

FOREWORD

Anyone who has ever studied with a great teacher knows how much power there is in the words of someone who truly knows his field. A brilliant artist describing the principles of painting, a distinguished physicist explaining quantum mechanics, a chess master discussing his game all speak with the assurance of having fully traversed a particular terrain and made it their own. When we work with such experts, we not only learn their subject, we absorb something of their expertise, something of the passion with which they have pursued it. Often, the sheer presence that infuses their words can help us understand things in a completely new way.

The power that lies in the words of a great spiritual teacher has something in common with the power we find in the words of other experts. A spiritual master has fully explored his territory; he has made it his own, and he speaks with the conviction of someone who knows what he is talking about. But the power in his words goes beyond the power of expertise. A spiritual master is a conqueror of the inner world of a human being, the complex, subtle, and infinitely difficult terrain of what is called the spiritual path. The artist, the physicist, or the chess master may be a failure in private life, as if his passionate concentration in one area had been achieved at the expense of the rest. But a spiritual master is by definition a master of the whole of life. He has freed himself from limitation in all its forms, and he demonstrates to us, by his example as well as his words, our own limitless possibilities for freedom and happiness. He shows us, in short, our own inner perfection. Contact with such a master can transform our lives.

Swami Muktananda is one of those rare teachers who possess that transforming authority. Muktananda is a Siddha. The term "Siddha" means "perfected one," and in the culture from which Muktananda comes it is applied only to men and women who have attained a state of total immersion in the inner Self, the state that mystics of all traditions consider the highest achievement possible for a human being. Not only is a Siddha established in that state, but he also has the ability to pass on the experience of it to others by awakening their inner spiritual energy, the Kundalini. So a Siddha master is not merely a teacher or a guide; he is a kind of spiritual touchstone, a catalytic force, the instigator and nourisher of the most profound growth process of which a human being is capable.

This growth process sometimes begins in extraordinarily dramatic ways. Early in 1981, a letter appeared in a south Florida journal from an inmate of one of the toughest penitentiaries in the state. He told the story of how, several years before, he had been on his way to kill a prison dope dealer who had cheated him on a deal. Carrying a homemade knife and seething with anger, the prisoner was walking down the corridor toward the dealer's cell, when he ran into a group of non-inmates standing around a man dressed in orange clothes. The man was Swami Muktananda, who had come to the prison to give a lecture. As the prisoner passed, his eyes caught Muktananda's, and in that moment he was seized with a strong and utterly unexpected sensation of love. The desire to kill the dope dealer simply left him, and he followed the group to the prison auditorium. He sat there for an hour listening to Muktananda talk about how, by his own thoughts and actions, a person can turn even a prison into a paradise. He received Muktananda's mantra that afternoon, and later began meditating regularly and corresponding with some of Muktananda's disciples. Over the next few years, his attitude toward himself and his life changed. Instead of feeling angry, desperate, and out of control, he found himself coming more and more in touch with an inner center of calm and clarity, a center that was unaffected by the harshness and agitation of prison life.

Although most people's initial contact with Muktananda does not occur under such dramatic circumstances, this incident is typical of the way in which a Siddha can connect us with our own center, our inner Self. The Self is the still point of our being, the part of us which remains somehow separate from the chaos of thoughts and feelings that ordinarily fills even the most well-ordered mind. That Self, as Muktananda tells us in these pages, is an enormous reservoir of joy, intelligence, and power, and it is also the most familiar part of us—so familiar, in fact, that we do not even notice it is there. And although most of us intuit the existence within ourselves of a potential for strength, fearlessness, and love far beyond what we normally experience, we come in contact with this potential only at moments—in times of danger or crisis, for example, or when we fall in love.

The key to unlocking our potential is spiritual practice, the process which in the Sanskrit language is called *sadhana.* This is a book about that process, which, as Muktananda teaches it, is not just a series of exercises or techniques, but a dynamic inner unfoldment that happens spontaneously once one's inner energy is awakened by a Siddha master.

Muktananda's path, Siddha Yoga, is the experiential aspect of a precise science of the spirit, evolved over centuries by men and women who used their own bodies as laboratories to research the subtle workings of the human consciousness and whose findings took form as the Upanishads, the *Bhagavad Gita,* the texts of yoga, and the great philosophical systems of Vedanta and Kashmir Shaivism. Like those of his ancient predecessors, Swami Muktananda's teachings come out of a lifetime of painstaking inner research, out of years of testing the words of the sages against his own experience in meditation. So when Muktananda declares that everything in the universe is made of divine Consciousness and that this Consciousness lives in the innermost core of an individual, when he tells us that God dwells within us as our own Self, he is not simply repeating what he read in a book; he is talking about something that is his own day-to-day experience. Whatever he teaches is what he himself has lived and knows at the deepest level of being.

Swami Muktananda was born in 1908 into a wealthy family in the south of India. At the age of fifteen, a few months after first meeting the saint who was later to become his Guru, he left home. He took vows as a monk, and for the next twenty-five years wandered up and down India, mostly on foot, studying the great spiritual texts of his tradition and mastering the different branches of yogic science. He was possessed with a desire for the ultimate experience, the realization of God, and he knew that traditionally one obtains that experience only through the agency of a master. To that end, he visited over sixty saints and stayed with many. By his thirties, he had become an accomplished yogi with enough spiritual power to attract many devotees in the towns and villages where he stayed. Yet he kept wandering, unsatisfied with his accomplishments. He was nearly forty by the time he again met Nityananda, a near-naked, often silent, and highly unconventional holy man who is considered one of India's greatest modern saints. Nityananda belonged to the original lineage of Siddha masters, and it was from Nityananda that Muktananda received *shaktipat,* the transmission of spiritual power which initiated in him the process of Siddha Yoga. After nine years of intense meditation under Nityananda's guidance, Muktananda reached his goal. It is said that one morning in 1956 Nityananda suddenly got up from his chair and began to dance, saying, "Muktananda is no longer Muktananda; he has become the Absolute!" His words were interpreted by the people who heard them as a kind of diploma, the teacher's assertion that his student had completed the course.

When Nityananda died in 1961, he passed on the power of the Siddha lineage to Muktananda. Taking on the succession did not at first change Muktananda's life—the passing on of Guruship is not a ceremonial act, and there was no investiture nor much public recognition, except among the inner circle of disciples. And in 1965, when the first Westerners began coming to Muktananda's ashram, they found it a tiny place, almost empty except when the crowds of devotees came on Sunday from Bombay. Muktananda never lectured in those days. If people asked questions about spiritual matters, he would answer them, but most of the time he sat silent or talked about the weather or the events of the village. Nothing was ever translated. But when visitors sat with him, they often found their minds becoming still, found themselves without warning or explanation falling into deep meditative states during which they saw visions and inner lights, or floated on waves of intense love, or experienced startling insights into the nature of reality. So year after year, as his ashram and his reputation grew, the Westerners kept coming back, and eventually persuaded him to visit their own countries.

He came to the West for the first time in 1970 and stayed for three months, traveling to cities like New York, San Francisco, and Paris. It was during this time that word began to get around about Muktananda's ability to infect people with his energy. Accounts circulated, too, about the changes that occurred in people's lives after they met him: how they spontaneously stopped smoking cigarettes or taking pills, how their damaged marriages were repaired, how their personal and professional lives took on new energy and direction. Even in those days it was clear that Muktananda's teaching, although delivered in a language resonant with traditional Eastern references, was genuinely universal, as applicable to a French lawyer or an engineer from Ohio as to an Indian yogi, and as true in New York as in Bombay. Not only was it universal, it was demonstrable. The statement that within every human being is divinity, which delivered by a lesser teacher might have seemed a mere spiritual truism, became actual experience for people whose inner energy was activated through *shaktipat.* Over the years, as Muktananda returned more frequently to the West, there grew up in his wake several hundred residential ashrams and meditation centers. Yet the greater part of his rapidly growing following in the West as well as in India consisted of working and professional people—doctors, teachers, carpenters, scientists, and a few politicians and movie stars—people who had learned that the process of Siddha Yoga, once begun, integrated itself very naturally into lives that also included work, friends, and family.

The idea that spiritual practice is not separate from ordinary life, but a part of it, is basic to Muktananda's teaching. Siddha Yoga, he explains, does not take place outside the context of our daily activities. The word he most often uses to describe the path he teaches is "natural." Just as physical growth takes place on its own and cannot be hurried or forced, the inner growth process of Siddha Yoga occurs spontaneously, gradually but inevitably leading to the experience of the Self. It is nourished by a moderate life style and the regular practice of meditation and mantra repetition, yet even the practice of these disciplines becomes easy once the awakened energy begins working. One of the most unusual aspects of Siddha Yoga is that it not only gives rise to spiritual experiences, but also creates the desire to lead a disciplined spiritual life. It is this phenomenon which accounts for the startling transformations that often occur in people who have come in contact with Muktananda. There are people who, a few days after meeting Muktananda, suddenly find themselves waking up at an hour when they might once have gone to bed, feeling a strong desire to meditate. There are others who find the mantra coming up in their minds while they are washing the dishes or riding to the office.

But by far the most important effect of Siddha Yoga is not the occurrence of spiritual phenomena, but the development of spiritual understanding, the understanding of our oneness with the Self. No matter what Muktananda is discussing in this book—whether he is delineating the theory of mantra, describing how to deal with unwanted thoughts, or explaining how to incorporate meditation into daily life, the key he offers is this understanding of oneness. It alone, he tells us, can free us of fear, can make us aware of our true relationship with one another, can help us through the ups and downs of life and bring us finally to the goal of the spiritual journey. "When you come to the end of your *sadhana,* you will realize that everything is the Self," Muktananda writes. "When this is the case, why do you not remember it now and meditate with the awareness that everything you see, inside and outside, is that

Self?" Sometimes humorously, sometimes cajolingly, sometimes sharply, he reminds us again and again that our true identity is not with the body or the mind, but with the Self, that infinitely creative, infinitely potent, infinitely joyful Consciousness which he knows and would have us know is the ground and essence of our being. Only when we understand that Consciousness, he tells us, do we understand what it is to be truly human. Only when we discover it within ourselves do we discover the meaning in our lives.

The process of coming to that discovery is the real theme of this book. *Where Are You Going?* is composed of essays, questions and answers, and interviews, which have been organized into chapters that together form a map of the journey of Self-knowing, as well as a basic introduction to Swami Muktananda's teachings. It presents not only the philosophy of Siddha Yoga, but also its essential practices, making it clear that the practices should not be mistaken for the process itself, but rather should be considered the means by which we fuel it and keep it going. Each chapter discusses a different facet of the path, weaving together basic themes and introducing new ones, covering the stages of the spiritual journey from the first understanding of its purpose to the achievement of the state of perfect freedom and joy which is its goal.

SALLY KEMPTON

SWAMI MUKTANANDA

WHERE ARE YOU GOING?

O my blessed beloved, awake!
Why do you sleep in ignorance?

— Kabir

The Purpose of Our Lives

O friend, where are you going? Where have you come from, and what are you supposed to do? You belong to the supreme Truth, but you have forgotten your origin. Now it is time to get back on the main road.

Today the world is said to be making more and more progress, but in what way has it become greater? Murder, thievery, fighting, and destruction are on the rise everywhere. All over the world there is hatred among nations, hostility among political parties, animosity among societies, and enmity among races and classes. People talk about innovation and reform, but in the name of these things they have succeeded only in destroying the environment, in wrecking family life, and in increasing selfishness and hostility.

In such a world there is only one thing we need, and that is the true understanding of humanity. Yet that is exactly what we lack. Why does a human being behave as he does? Why does he create barriers between himself and others? Why does he live with enmity and competition instead of a feeling of brotherhood? He does these things because he lacks true understanding about himself. He does not know the greatness that lies within the human heart. He imagines that he is false, ordinary, and weak and that he will simply pass through this world and die. Yet if he were to look within himself, he would realize that he contains the divinity of the entire world.

Western scientists are now beginning to discover the truth that the philosophers of India have known for millennia: that the entire universe consists of one energy. Our ancient philosophers, who were scientists of the spirit, called that energy Consciousness, or God. This supreme Consciousness created the entire cosmos out of its own being.[1] A builder may use wood, stone, and other materials to construct something, but Consciousness used no external material; it brought forth everything from within itself. We are all portions of this universe of Consciousness. We are not different from one another, and we are not different from God. If one sows a mango seed one will get a mango, never a lemon. In the same way, that which is born of God can never be other than God. Within the human heart dwells a shimmering effulgence whose brilliance surpasses even that of the sun. This inner Consciousness is the same as that which creates and animates the entire universe. But we are not aware of this. Even though we have come from this Consciousness, we have changed our understanding about ourselves.

Once, when I was in Bombay, I heard some children singing a song from a movie, and I remember it to this day:

> O man, how did you change?
> The earth has not changed, water has not changed.
> Fire has not changed, air and ether have not changed.
> The sun has not changed, the moon has not changed.
> Animals have not changed, trees have not changed.
> O man, how did you change?

How did we change? Every one of us has become one thing or another, according to our own understanding. We believe ourselves to be men or women, rich people or poor people. We believe that we are teachers, soldiers, psychiatrists. We believe that we are young or old, fat or thin, happy or miserable. We believe that we are Americans or Indians, Russians or Arabs, Hindus or Christians, Muslims or Jews. But in reality, the Truth within us is one. We all come from the same seed, and that seed is God. We are simply playing different roles. If we could only penetrate beneath these roles to our own divinity, then once again we would all know that we are God.

The Freedom to Become

A human being has the freedom to become anything. By his own power he can make his life sublime or wretched. By his own power he can reach the heavens or descend to the depths. In fact, the power of a human being is so great that he can even transform himself into God. God lies hidden in the heart of every human being, and everyone has the power to realize that. But what does a person do? Instead of trying to know the greatness within himself, he spends his life eating and drinking, fighting with others, and chasing after the pleasures of the senses. He makes two or three children, takes care of his family, and thinks he has fulfilled the purpose of his life. But even animals do these things. Every creature in the world eats and drinks. Every creature in the world has a family life. An animal goes into the jungle, does his work, and comes back to enjoy his animal mate and offspring. In the same way, a human being goes into the world, attends to his business, comes back, and enjoys his family. Just as the progeny of human beings continue to increase, the number of dogs, donkeys, elephants, camels, horses, and birds also continues to grow. This is why Pooli, a great woman saint, said, "If you do not attain your own Self, if you do not experience supreme bliss, then what is the use of living? Do not dogs and pigs also live? Do not trees also live? Do not rocks also exist in this world?"

What is it, then, that makes a human being unique? Only a human being has the capacity to know the divine Consciousness vibrating within him. Only a human being has the ability to experience his identity with God. That is why we must use this human life to discover who we are. The Indian scriptures say that only one who contemplates the questions "Who am I?" "Why was I born?" "Who created me?" and "What am I supposed to do?" is truly human.[2] If a person does not know his own Self, if his understanding of himself is restricted to knowledge of his flesh, then he cannot be called a true human being. The great saint Kabir said, "If you have not seen your own Self, if you have not pierced the knots of your heart and washed away the filth of your mind, then what does it really matter if you are a human being?"

The Value of Human Birth

We should understand the value of human birth. We consider human life to be very cheap since it is so easy for us to make children, and even after having obtained this body most of us spend our lives satisfying our senses. But the human body is priceless. The sages have said that human birth is very rare.[3] Only after passing through thousands of life forms do we obtain this body.

Once a disciple of Guru Nanakdev asked him, "What is the value of a human being?" The saint said, "Come back tomorrow, and I will tell you." The next morning when the disciple returned, Guru Nanakdev handed him a diamond with the instructions, "Take this to the market and have it appraised. Do not sell it; just take it to every shopkeeper and get a price for it."

The disciple took the diamond from shopkeeper to shopkeeper. First, he went to the fruit seller. "How much will you give me for this?" he asked. "I will give you two oranges," said the fruit seller. Next he went to the potato seller, who said, "I will give you four kilos of potatoes." Then the disciple went to a goldsmith, a very ordinary jeweller, and asked him to price the diamond. "I will give you one hundred dollars," said the goldsmith. The disciple went to several other jewellers, each of whom offered him a little more money. Finally he went to the best jeweller in town and asked him to price the diamond. The jeweller placed the diamond on his palm. "O brother," he said, "you cannot sell this diamond. It is priceless."

The disciple brought the diamond back to Nanakdev and told him what had happened. "Now do you understand the value of a human being?" Nanakdev asked. "A person can sell himself for two oranges or four kilos of potatoes or, if he likes, he can make himself priceless. It all depends on his own vision."

The great saint Sunderdas wrote, "You have attained this human body through God's grace. You cannot attain it over and over again. O forgetful one, remember! This human body is a priceless jewel. Do not throw it away."

You will discover the value of this body when you see your own inner Self. The human body is a temple within which

God dwells in the form of the Self. However, to know this, you must turn within through meditation. In your present state, you have only partial awareness. You know the world only as it appears in the waking state. You do not know what lies beyond it, even though every night you experience a world beyond your ordinary awareness. When you are awake, whatever you see around you is real for you. But when you fall asleep and dream, the waking world ceases to exist, and the world of dreams becomes real.

In ancient India there was a sovereign named Janaka who was also a great man of knowledge. One day after lunch he was taking a nap in his flower-strewn bed. His servants were fanning him, and his guards were standing at attention. As he slept, Janaka dreamed that a neighboring king attacked him and defeated him in battle. The victorious king told Janaka that he was free to go anywhere, as long as he left the kingdom. Weary from fighting, Janaka fled his kingdom and soon began to starve. As he wandered, he came upon a field of corn, picked two ears, and began to eat them. Just then the owner of the field came by and saw a strange man helping himself to his corn. He took out a whip and beat the king severely.

As soon as he received those blows, Janaka woke up. He sat up and saw that he was still in his bed, that his servants were still fanning him, and that his guards were still standing at attention. So he lay down and closed his eyes. Once again he was in the field, being beaten by the farmer. He opened his eyes and saw that he was still lying in his bed. Then he began to wonder, "Which of these is real, my dream or what I am seeing now? I must have an answer to this."

He sent a message throughout the kingdom asking all the great scholars, sages, seers, psychics, inventors, and scientists to come to the palace and answer his question. When they had all assembled, he asked them, "Tell me which is real, the waking state or the dream state?" But no one knew how to answer the question. If they called the dream state real, they would have to call the waking state unreal, but if they called the waking state real, they would have to call the dream state unreal. The king became enraged. "I have been feeding all of you for so many years," he said, "but you cannot give me an answer to a simple question. All you have been doing is getting fat." He ordered them to be locked in the royal prison. Then he had his question posted in public places throughout the kingdom: "Which of these states is real—dream or waking? Anyone who knows the answer to this question should come to the palace and explain it to me."

Many days passed. One of the sages had a son named Ashtavakra. The name means "deformed in eight places," for Ashtavakra had been born with a completely crooked body. One day he asked his mother, "Where is my father?"

His mother replied, "He is in the king's jail."

"Why? Did he steal something?"

"No," she said. "He wasn't able to answer the king's question, so he was thrown in jail."

"I can answer the question," Ashtavakra said, and he went directly to the king's palace. Outside the palace was a huge drum, and next to it was a sign saying that anyone who wanted to answer the king's question should strike it. Ashtavakra beat the drum. The palace door opened, and he was taken inside to the king's reception hall.

When the royal courtiers saw Ashtavakra walking into the hall, they all began to laugh. They were amused that this misshapen boy should consider himself capable of answering the king's question when all the learned men of the kingdom had been unable to do so. When Ashtavakra saw them, he began to laugh too.

The king said, "The courtiers are laughing because you walk in such a peculiar way and also because you are so young. But tell me, why are you laughing?"

Ashtavakra answered, "Your Majesty, I had heard that you and your courtiers were enlightened people, but now I see how stupid you are. You laugh at my deformities, which are only skin-deep. But all bodies are made of the same five elements. If you were to look at me from the point of view of the Self, you would see that the Self is also the same in everyone and that there is nothing to laugh at. And as for your question, O king, neither the waking state nor the dream state is real. When you are awake, the world of dreams does not exist, and when you dream, the waking world does not exist. Therefore, neither can be true."

The king asked, "If both the waking and dream states are unreal, what *is* real?"

"There is another state beyond those states," Ashtavakra replied. "Discover that state. It alone is real."

The Four States

Like King Janaka, we know only the ordinary states of consciousness in which we live; we do not have complete knowledge of reality. When we are awake, we are totally immersed in our waking world. When we dream, our activities, our world, and our understanding are completely different than when we are awake. When we go into the state of deep sleep, we lose consciousness altogether. But when we meditate, we pass even beyond the deep sleep state and enter the state of the Self. That state is the foundation of all the other states, and it alone is permanent and unchanging.[4] Once we enter this state, we will experience the truth about ourselves. We will realize that we are nothing but Consciousness. This physical body is like the clothes we wear. Just as they are merely a covering for the body, in the same way the physical body is merely a covering for our innermost Consciousness. To know that Consciousness is the purpose of our lives.

If everyone could experience that inner Truth, if everyone could understand his real nature, there would no longer be enmity among people, but only friendliness, affection, and the feeling of universal brotherhood. For this reason, it is absolutely necessary that we come to know the Self. Only when we know our own Self can we know others. Only when we see the greatness that exists within us can we see the greatness in others. When we look at ourselves with the true awareness of humanity, we will see that same humanity in everyone else, and then we will realize that everyone in this world is a child of God.

The Pursuit of Happiness

The Indian scriptures pose a major question: "What is the purpose of human life?" According to the sages of Vedanta, the aim of life is to eliminate all suffering and to attain the highest joy. If we think about it, we will realize that everything we do in life we do for the sake of these two things. What do we want? We want happiness. We want ecstasy. We want love, vigor, and enthusiasm. And in one way or another we try to obtain these things. For the sake of happiness we fall in love, get married, and raise children. For the sake of happiness we do business, earn money, accumulate possessions, and pursue various talents, skills, and entertainments. Even when we deceive and harm other people, we do it with the hope that it will bring us happiness. But if we were to truly examine ourselves, then we would discover that the happiness we are looking for can be found only within us. A poet-saint of Maharashtra wrote:

> O man, you have roamed so much in the outer world.
> You have gone from one place to another,
> You have picked flowers and fruit and pursued
>   countless activities,
> But all you have earned is weariness.
> Now it is time to soar in the boundless inner spaces.
> What you are seeking can be found there
>   in its fullness.

Why is it so difficult to turn within? We want happiness, yet we continually practice the yoga of pain. We sow the seeds of suffering and then wonder when the fruit of happiness is going to blossom.

I travel from one country to another, and I meet people from every different field. I meet rich people and poor people, and everyone tells me the same story. Everyone is unhappy. Yet no matter how dissatisfied people are with their lives, they keep doing exactly what they have been doing all along. They never stop to think how they might put an end to their troubles. Instead, they merely complain, blaming their husband or wife, their boss, the government, or the times. They think, "If only I could get him to love me, I would be so happy." "If only I had a better job, there would be no more suffering in my life." "If only she behaved the way I wanted her to, everything would be blissful." And in this way, their days go by.

Bravely Eating Chilis

There is a story that illustrates this predicament very well. Once Sheikh Nasrudin visited India. While roaming through the city of Delhi, he came upon a vegetable and fruit market. As he stood in the market watching, he noticed that many people were buying chilis. In India people are very fond of chilis, but they use them in small quantities. Nasrudin thought they must be a delicacy, so he bought two kilos of them, and sat down under a tree to eat them. As he munched the first chili, his mouth began to burn, and his eyes and nose began to water. He moaned and fanned his mouth, and then began munching another chili, thinking that this one would taste better. He went on in this way, eating chili after chili, suffering and hoping that each one would taste better than the last. We are just like Nasrudin. We are all eating chilis in the hope that the chili we eat tomorrow—or if not that one, certainly the one we eat the day after—will taste better. We keep offering the same chilis to each other, hoping that someday, somewhere, they will start to taste sweet. But the fact is that at the present moment our mouths are burning, our eyes are watering, and our noses are running.

While Nasrudin was bravely munching his chilis, a man who had been watching walked up to him and asked what he was doing. "I saw a lot of people buying this delicacy, so I also bought some and began to eat them," explained Nasrudin.

The man said, "Look, these are chilis. They are supposed to be eaten in very small quantities." Nasrudin nodded and went on eating. The man was astonished. "Now that you know what they are," he said, "why don't you stop eating them?"

"Well," said Nasrudin, "I bought these chilis, and I have to finish them. I'm not eating chilis any longer. I'm eating my money!"

This is how we live our lives. We have bought our problems, and even though we find them quite hot, we have to go on eating them because we have made the investment. We keep searching for more fun, more entertainment, more loving friends, more wealth, more fame. But do any of these things bring us real satisfaction? Do our enjoyments bring us true joy, or do they bring us only dryness and heat? What are we really accomplishing in our pursuit of satisfaction?

The poet Bartruhari wrote:

> I thought I was enjoying sense pleasures; I did not realize
> they were enjoying me.
> I thought I was spending my time; I did not realize
> it was spending me.[5]

Look at your life. Open your eyes. While you have pursued the fulfillment of your desires, time has eaten you up.

It is the nature of desire to expand. The more we pursue our desires, the more they increase. No matter what we have in the world, we always want more. If we have a dollar, we want ten dollars. If we have ten dollars, we want one hundred dollars. If we have a Volkswagen, we want a Mercedes. If we have one drink, we want another. But until we turn within and discover the satisfaction of the Self, we will have no lasting satisfaction, no matter how much money we acquire, no matter how many friends we accumulate, no matter how much we accomplish in the world. All the joys of the outer world are temporary. They can never last. In fact, without the joy of the Self, our mundane joys are like a string of zeros without a number one preceding them to give them value. Without the joy of the Self, our wealth is zero, our beauty is zero, and our accomplishments are zero. Only when we drink the nectar of the Self do all our zeros amount to something.

The Dog's Bone

Happiness is within us, and it is ours, but we are always superimposing our own inner joy onto something outside and thinking it comes from there. If you examine your actions very subtly, you will find that even your mundane joy comes not from the objects of enjoyment but from within you. You say, "I feel so good when I listen to music. I get so much happiness from playing tennis." But actually, when you do these things, it is your own inner joy that you experience. In Vedanta there is a proverb: "The joy of the world is like a dog's bone." A dog finds a piece of bone and starts to chew on it. As he chews, pieces of the bone get stuck in his gums and blood begins to flow. The dog tastes the blood and thinks, "This bone is delicious!" The more he chews on the bone, the more his gums bleed. The more he tastes the blood, the sweeter he feels the bone to be. This is an unending cycle. Just as the dog does not realize that he is tasting his own blood, you do not realize that the joy you get from this world is coming from inside you.

Think about the happiness you find in your life. Where does it come from? When you have finished eating and your stomach is full, you experience a moment of satisfaction. When you meet a friend after a long time and embrace him, you feel joy for a fraction of a moment. When an artist contemplates his work, he experiences a few seconds of peace. What actually happens at such moments is that the mind becomes still, and the center of bliss within reveals itself, like a flash of lightning. Yet the bliss you experience then is not everlasting, and it is just a shadow of the bliss inside. To experience this bliss directly, you must turn within in meditation and look for happiness where it really dwells.

The problem is that you do not want to look within. Your camera records only what is going on in the outer world; it never turns around and records what is going on inside. Yet every night you experience the benefits of turning within. During the day, you accumulate so many things, see so many friends, work so hard, and enjoy so many pleasures. You do all these things for the sake of happiness, but at the end of the day you come home and say, "I feel tired." No matter what you do during the day, whether you earn a million dollars, attain the highest title, or go to a fabulous party, when the day is over you feel exhausted, and then all you want to do is sleep. When the time comes to sleep, you have no use for any of the possessions you have worked so hard to accumulate during the day. You do not even want the people you love. All you want is rest. So you retire to a darkened room and wrap yourself in a warm blanket.

The next morning, if anyone asks you how you feel, you say, "I'm full of energy." A few hours of sleep have completely refreshed you. You have not eaten anything, done anything, bought anything, or enjoyed anything, yet you feel completely rejuvenated. This is your daily experience. Why is it that the activities you enjoy so much during the day make you tired, while a few hours of sleep make you so strong and energetic? Your own sleep teaches you over and over again that the real source of strength and energy is within you.

The Inner World

If during the day you could go within and meditate just for a while, you could tap that source, and then you would remain in a state of continual enthusiasm and joy. Inside everyone is a divine, conscious energy called Kundalini. Through meditation, this inner energy is awakened and makes a spontaneous yoga unfold within. Most people think that yoga consists of the physical movements of hatha yoga, but the true meaning of yoga is "reunion"—the reunion with the Self from which you have become separated. When the inner energy is awakened and this spontaneous yoga begins, your entire body will be purified from within. Your awareness will turn inside, and you will be able to see the inner worlds. Eventually, through the meditation that takes place after the awakening of the inner energy, you will recognize your true nature, your own inner Self. You will reach a center which is beyond pleasure and pain, a state in which you will experience nothing but bliss. That is the state of the Self.

When you see the Self, when you experience it, you will be completely transformed. The world, too, will be transformed for you, and you will see it in an entirely different way. There is a saying: "What is day for a crow is night for an owl." In the same way, the world which is filled with so many difficulties and complications for an ignorant person is heaven for a person who knows the Self. God is filled with virtues, with beauty, and with many great skills, and He has placed them within all of us. But you cannot see them just by reveling in the outer world. You have to attain a subtle eye in order to perceive the inner principle.

You have no idea of the vastness that exists inside you. This body seems small, yet it is an image of the entire universe. In this body is a sun one thousand times more brilliant than the outer sun and yet, instead of being hot, it is cooling. Because of that inner light, which resides in the *sahasrara,* the great spiritual center in the crown of the head, you have luster on your face and radiance in your eyes. In the heart is a center of knowledge, within which you can see the entire world. In fact, there are so many things inside you that I could write volumes describing them. All the wonders you see in the outer world can be found to a far greater degree within. All the pleasures you look for can be discovered in far greater measure inside.

Throughout your life you try to gratify your eyes with beautiful sights, to delight your ears with melodious sounds, to please your nose with exquisite fragrances, your skin with sweet touch, and your tongue with new tastes. Out of longing to hear sweet music, you listen to rock and roll, to symphonies, or to opera. But when the inner energy awakens and rises to the *sahasrara,* you will hear divine sounds that are so sweet they cannot be described. As you listen to them, you will become increasingly happy, and even your physical ailments will be cured.

When this music resounds in the inner spaces, a divine nectar will drip down onto the tongue. You are always looking for tasty food and drink. For the sake of delicious tastes you eat so many different dishes; for the sake of flavor you drink so many beverages. But when you drink that inner nectar, you will find it so delicious that no outer taste will compare with it.

In the same way, you enjoy fragrance. You apply perfume to your body in order to smell sweet, but as old age comes, your body itself begins to stink. However, when you go deep within in meditation, exquisite fragrances will begin to fill your being, fragrances so sweet that, as you smell them, your mind will become still.

You also long for touch. To experience the joy of touch, you embrace and rub your body against other bodies, until finally your sense of touch gets worn out and you can no longer feel anything. But when the inner energy is awakened, it will begin to play within you, and then your entire being will experience the thrill of its subtle touch. You will be filled with the most exquisite sensations, and you will become completely satisfied.

Moreover, you yearn to look at beautiful forms and to make your own form beautiful. To make your body attractive, you put powders and creams on your face, but in time the chemicals begin to affect the skin, and then without makeup you look like a ghost. You comb your hair and decorate yourself with beautiful clothes, but your clothes get dirty and wear out. In this way, outer beauty is transitory; it is there for a moment, and then it eludes you. But inner beauty is unchanging. It never ages, and it is never spoiled. As you meditate more and more, as the inner energy works within, you will begin to perceive such beauty that you will hardly have the strength to bear it. In the center of the brilliant effulgence in the *sahasrara* is a tiny, sparkling blue light known as the blue pearl. That is the light of the Self within you. Seeing it, the great Siddhas have declared, "God dwells within every human being."

Everything you seek in this world is within you. Supreme joy blazes inside. But it is not enough merely to have an intellectual understanding of this. You have to go deep inside; you have to dig it out. Then you will see the scintillating Consciousness that lives within you in the form of bliss. The great Sufi saint Mansur Mastana said, "You can break a temple, you can break a mosque. You can break Kaab'a, you can break Kiibli'i. But never break a human heart, because in the heart God dwells." The heart is the true house of God. It is the seat of happiness, the abode of unending love. Go there.

The Bee and the Elephant

Once there was a bee who was young and strong and full of the hot blood of youth. One day he was flying blissfully from flower to flower, sucking nectar. He kept going farther from home, forgetting that it would soon be evening and time to return.

He had just flown into a lotus flower when the sun set and the lotus closed. The bee was trapped. He had a sharp stinger and could easily have pierced through the petals and flown away, but he was lost in his intoxication. He thought, "I'll spend the night here drinking nectar, and in the morning, when the lotus opens, I'll fly home. I'll get my wife and my neighbors and friends and bring them here to drink nectar. They will be so pleased! They will be so grateful!"

Soon it was midnight. There was a young elephant roaming through the forest, and he was also very intoxicated. He was tearing down trees and ripping up plants and stuffing them into his mouth. When he came to the lake where the bee was reveling, he began to snatch the lotuses and eat them. The bee was still drinking nectar and thinking, "I will bring my wife. I will bring my neighbors. I will bring all my friends. I will have a great honey factory." Suddenly there was a loud crunch. "Alas!" the bee cried. "I am dying. I am dying. I am dead."

All the bee's plans remained in the lake. All his friends remained in their houses. His wife was still at home. And the bee was inside the elephant's mouth.

Like that bee, we are going farther and farther in this world, imagining that we are making greater and greater progress, not realizing that we are leaving our source behind. Every day, the elephant of death comes closer, but we never notice his footsteps.

This world is transitory. Although it seems bewitching, everything we see here is perishable. The great saint Kabir sang, "You are like a traveler who comes and goes. You accumulate wealth and take pride in your riches. But when you leave, you will take nothing with you. You came into this world with your fists clenched, but when you go, your hands will be open." In this world everything changes, everything decays. Youth becomes old age, health becomes sickness, beauty becomes disease. Kabir said, "As you watch it, your life turns to dust." A time will come when every empire, monument, and city will crumble. There have been so many kings, emperors, and great leaders, but where have they gone? Only the inner Self is eternal. Only the inner Consciousness will last.

Without meditation on the Self, without spiritual practice, the only thing you will attain is your death. Most people think that youth is a time for eating, drinking, and indulging in all the pleasures of the world, and that when their bodies have become old and worn out they can start thinking of God. But what can you do when your body is old? Once your house is on fire, what is the use of digging a well? For this reason, the poet Bartruhari wrote, "As long as your body is healthy and strong, as long as your senses still function, do something for yourself." Why wait? Contemplate the Self and attain it now. Know that life is very short. You were not born into this world just to eat and drink and die.

Notes

1. Kshemaraja, *Pratyabhijnahridayam: Svecchayā svabitau vishvam unmīlayati* —"[Universal Consciousness] unfolds this universe upon Her own screen."
2. See Shankaracharya, *Aparokshanubhuti.*
3. See Shankaracharya, *Vivekachudamani (The Crest-Jewel of Discrimination),* v.2: *Durlabham traya mevetad devanugraha hetukam manushaytam mumukshutvam mahāpurusha samshrayaha* —"There are three things which are rare indeed and are due to the grace of God — namely, a human birth, the longing for liberation, and the protecting care of a perfected sage."
4. See *Shiva Sutras,* I.7: *Jāgratsvapnasushuptabhede turyābhoga sambhavaha* — "Even during the three different states of consciousness, in waking, dreaming, and deep sleep, the rapturous experience of 'I'-consciousness of the fourth state abides." See Shankaracharya, *Vivekachudamani,* v. 90– 107, for a description of the three states of waking, dreaming, and deep sleep and *Mandukya Upanishad* for a description of the four states.
5. Bartruhari, *Vairagya Shataka.*

The Self

Smaller than the smallest,
  greater than the greatest,
This Self forever dwells
  in the hearts of all.
A person freed from desire,
  with mind and senses purified,
Beholds the glory of the Self
  and is without sorrow.

— Katha Upanishad

The Source of All Our Joy

Nothing in the world is greater than the Self. All our joy, all our inspiration, and all our strength come from the Self. In fact, the Self contains everything in the universe. You will experience this when you turn within and see it in meditation.

Yajnavalkya was one of the greatest sages of ancient times. He had two wives: Katyayani, who was old, and Maitreyi, who was very young. One day Yajnavalkya called both wives and told them, "I am giving up this household life and going into the forest to live as a renunciant. I have divided my wealth into two shares, and I am giving one share to each of you."

The older wife accepted her share, but Maitreyi asked, "Why are you giving up your wealth and going away?"

"Because the Self cannot be satisfied with wealth," Yajnavalkya replied.

"Will this wealth give me immortality?" she asked.

"No," said Yajnavalkya. "Your life will be like that of the rich. No one can possibly hope to attain immortality through wealth."

"Then I do not want it," said Maitreyi. "I married you in your old age not for the sake of your wealth, but for the sake of your knowledge. I want to attain the Self."

Yajnavalkya was very pleased by this. "O Maitreyi," he said, "you were always dear to me, but now you are dearer."

"Give all your material wealth to Katyayani," Maitreyi said. "Give me the wealth of your knowledge."

In response, Yajnavalkya began to explain the greatness of the Self to her. "O Maitreyi," he said, "we love one another not for each other's sake, but for the sake of the Self. A husband is dear to his wife not for his own sake, but for the sake of the Self. A wife is dear to her husband not for her own sake, but for the sake of the Self. All creatures are dear to us not for their own sake, but for the sake of the Self. The Self is the dearest thing in the world.

"O Maitreyi, see the Self. Hear the Self. Contemplate the Self. Meditate on the Self. Make the Self manifest before you. By hearing about the essential nature of the Self, by contemplating and meditating on the essential nature of the Self, by perceiving the essential nature of the Self, you will come to know everything that can be known."[1]

The Pure "I"

What is the Self? It is the pure awareness of "I am," the original "I"-consciousness which has been within us ever since we came into this world. Even though that "I" exists in a woman, it is not a woman. Even though it exists in a man, it is not a man. That "I" is without form, color, or any other attribute. We have superimposed different notions onto it—notions like "I am a man," "I am a woman," "I am American." But when we wipe them all away, that "I" is nothing but pure Consciousness,[2] and it is the supreme Truth. Perceiving that "I," the great Shankaracharya proclaimed, *Aham brahmasmi*[3]—"I am the Absolute." Perceiving that "I," the great Sufi saint Mansur Mastana said, *Anal-haq*—"I am God."

That "I" is the source of this world. A banyan seed is tiny, and if you crack it open you will find nothing inside. Yet that seed contains an entire tree with its roots, branches, and leaves. In the same way, the Self is the seed which contains the whole universe.[4] Everything is within the Self, and therefore when we know the Self, we know everything that can be known. This is why the sages continually contemplate the Self, meditate on the Self, and lose themselves in the Self.

The power of the Self controls everything in the cosmos, and it is the same power which makes everything function within us.[5] Through the will of the Self, the breath moves in and out. Through the will of the Self, the mind moves to different objects. Because the Self exists, we can speak. Because the Self exists, we can understand one another's words.[6] Pulsating within, the power of the Self makes the senses conscious, enabling the eyes to see, the ears to hear, and the hands to grasp. Only because the Self exists inside us do we love each other; only because of the Self do we find each other radiant and beautiful. The moment the Self leaves it, the body becomes worthless and is thrown away.

The Self Is the True God

Without the knowledge of the Self, even the practice of religion will not take us to God. The great sages said that God is not found only in mosques, temples, or churches. God is the formless foundation of all. The Self is the true God,[7] and it is the basis of all religions and all modes of worship.

No matter how we worship God, it is the Self which gives us the fruit of that worship, for no matter what we love on the outside, the happiness we derive from it comes from within. For this reason, knowers of the Truth abandon all rituals and religions and worship the Self alone. When we know that everything comes from the Self, we realize that to worship anything but the Self is meaningless. At one time, I was a great worshipper of Shiva. Whenever I went to visit my Guru, I would go first to the Shiva temple near his ashram, and there I would perform worship by bathing the *lingam,* a representation of God's unmanifest form. One day when I went to my Guru he asked me, "O Muktananda, where have you been?"

"Worshipping Shiva," I said.

"Why do you worship Shiva outside?" he asked. "Shiva is within. Worship Him there."

A saint of India sang, "O man, you worship an idol made of stone, and that idol becomes God for you. Consciousness is within everything, so if you make an image of God and worship it, because of your feelings you will attain something. But

God lives inside you. When this is the case, if you worship your own Self will you not become God?"

The Nature of the Self

The Self is the most subtle of all subtle things. It is highly secret and mysterious, and it has no name, no color, and no form. Even though it is without attributes, the sages have described its nature as *satchidananda*—existence, consciousness, and bliss absolute.[8]

Sat means absolute Truth, the Truth that exists in all places, in all things, and at all times. If That were not omnipresent, it would not be the Truth; it would not have absolute existence. For instance, a chair that exists in New York does not exist in Los Angeles. It exists now, but it did not exist last year. So that chair does not have absolute existence. But the Self exists in the east, in the west, in the north, and in the south. It exists in all countries. It is here today, it was here yesterday, and it will be here tomorrow. The Self is not bound by any place, thing, or time. The sages of Kashmir Shaivism ask, "What time is there in which there is no Shiva?* What place is there in which there is no Shiva? What object is there in which there is no Shiva?" God, the Self, exists everywhere in His fullness.[9] Being present in everything, He is also present within us.

Chit is consciousness, which illumines everything. *Chit* makes us aware of all outer objects as well as our inner feelings. When we are upset or unhappy, consciousness illumines these feelings, and when we feel bliss, consciousness makes us aware of that, too. It makes us aware that God exists inside, and if we think that God does not exist because we have not seen Him, it is *chit* which gives rise to that understanding as well. *Chit* illumines that reality which exists in all places, all things, and all times. The Self is *chit,* and it illumines itself as well as everything else.

Ananda is bliss, and it can be understood only after we attain That. The nature of the Self as *sat* and *chit* can be dis-

---

*"Shiva" does not refer to the Hindu deity, but to the all-pervasive Consciousness, of which Shiva is one name.

cussed, but the bliss of the Self must be experienced in meditation. That bliss is far greater than the bliss which arises from seeing a beautiful form, hearing a melodious sound, tasting delicious food, or experiencing the softness of a touch. The pleasures born of the senses depend on the senses, and if the objects of pleasure disappear the bliss also disappears. But the bliss of the Self does not depend on any external factor. It is completely independent; it arises, unconditioned, from within. When the mind and intellect come close to the Self, they are able to experience that bliss. The great being Jnaneshwar Maharaj said, "The effulgence of the Self is ever-new." The bliss of the Self constantly renews itself. Sometimes, when I was wandering around India, I would come across great beings who laughed constantly, and I would wonder, "Don't they ever get tired of laughing?" Now I understand why they were always laughing. They would feel bliss and laugh, and in the next moment they would feel a new kind of bliss, so they would laugh again. Because their bliss was ever-new, they would keep laughing and laughing. One who depends on the senses for happiness is constantly looking for new things to satisfy him. He has to have new tastes, new music, new love. But since the bliss of the Self is always different, a yogi never gets tired of it.

The Self is our dearest friend. It exists inside us in its fullness, right within the heart. Though the Self is always with us, it is so subtle that most people cannot see or hear it. The Self is the formless substratum of everything,[10] the foundation of our lives. We cannot see it through the eyes, nor can we attain it through speech. The tongue can speak about it, but the true description of its nature is silence. The Self cannot be attained through the mind or through the senses. Yet when the inner psychic instruments are purified through meditation, it reveals itself on its own. For this reason, the sages of India place great emphasis on meditation; in the *Bhagavad Gita,* the Lord tells Arjuna, *Dhyānen ātmani pashyanti*[11] — "The Self is seen through meditation." Just by meditating peacefully, we can make the Self manifest before us.

The Inner Knower

I read a poem in which a great being said, "O my dear one, listen to my words. The wisdom of the Self is very easy to attain. Even if an ordinary person looks within through meditation, he will see the light of the Self." The Self is manifest; it is not concealed. The reason we cannot perceive it with our ordinary senses is that the Self is itself the perceiver.

Once someone asked a great sage, "What is that Self?" The sage replied, "The Self is the witness of the mind."[12] Within us is a being who observes all the activities of our waking hours. At night, when we go to sleep, that being does not sleep but stays awake and in the morning reports to us on our dreams. Who is that knower? The *Katha Upanishad* says that the one which perceives both dream and waking states is the all-pervasive Self.[13]

When Rama asked the sage Vasishtha, "What is the nature of the Self?" Vasishtha explained, "O Rama, that is the Self through which you perceive and discriminate among forms, flavors, smells, and touch. That is the Self through which you know the pleasure of the touch of love. That through which you know all things, O Rama, is the Self, which is the supreme Truth."[14]

In Kashmir Shaivism, it is said that the Self is *prakasha* and *vimarsha.*[15] These words are very significant. *Prakasha* means "light," and as *prakasha,* the Self illumines everything. For example, if there is a clay pot in front of us, it is *prakasha* which makes that pot reveal itself to us. *Vimarsha* means "awareness," and it is the power of understanding which makes us aware of what something is. When *prakasha* illumines the pot, *vimarsha* makes us realize that we are seeing a pot made of clay. *Prakasha* and *vimarsha* exist in everything, illuminating the outer world as well as the inner world. Being both *prakasha* and *vimarsha,* the Self illumines the mind, the intellect, and all the senses. In the *Bhagavad Gita,* Lord Krishna tells Arjuna, *Sarvendriyagunā bhāsam sarvendriyavivarjitam; / asaktam sarvabhricchaiva nirgunam gunabhoktru cha*[16]—"That shines through all our senses, yet is without senses. It supports the senses, yet remains apart from them. It experiences all the qualities of nature, yet remains detached from them." Whatever happens inside or outside, the Self sees and knows it. That Self, that Consciousness, is what comes to know itself through meditation.

The Rarest Gift

Even though the Self is always with us, knowledge of the Self is the rarest of gifts, and it comes only through the grace of God. To know the Self is to eliminate all one's suffering and to attain the highest bliss. Until the mind becomes pleased by merging into the Self, it constantly burns in the fire of attachment and aversion. But when one attains the Self, one attains its supremely free joy, which the pain of the world can never touch. From the womb of that bliss, a fountain of nectar arises. How can one who has attained this bliss ever hunger or thirst? How can one who understands his own Self ever suffer from the misery of the world? Therefore, for your own joy, seek the Self. Once you realize the glory of the Self, you will know that there is nothing greater.

God Has Never Left the Heart

In India there lived a great Sufi named Hazrat Basjid Bastami. When he was young, Bastami set out on a pilgrimage to Mecca. On his way, he came upon a dervish, an ecstatic being. "Where are you going?" the dervish asked.

"To Mecca," Bastami replied.

"Why?"

"To see God."

"How much money do you have?"

"Four hundred gold *dinars.*"

"Give them to me," said the dervish. He took the money and put it in his pocket. Then he said, "What will you do in Mecca? You will simply walk around the sacred rock seven times. Instead of doing that, walk around me seven times." Bastami did as he was told. "Now you can leave," the dervish said. "You have achieved your purpose. But first let me tell you something. Since the day Mecca was built, God has never dwelled there. But since the heart was created, God has never left it. Go home and meditate."

Whoever has attained God has attained Him within the human heart. The heart is the greatest temple of God.

Water in the River, Water in the Bowl

Q: What is the difference between the individual soul and the supreme soul?

SM: The individual soul and the supreme soul are not two different things; the individual soul is also the supreme soul. It is just that the supreme soul, God, has the awareness that it exists everywhere, whereas the individual soul believes that it exists only from head to toe. In reality there is no difference, but your understanding creates a difference. The reason for this is ignorance, which is lack of knowledge, or wrong understanding, of your own Self. When you obtain complete understanding of your Self, the idea of difference vanishes.

Once a Guru was explaining to his disciples, "God and the soul are one and the same. Just as God exists within Himself, He exists within all of us in the same measure."

One of his disciples got up and said, "O Guruji, God is so great. He has so much power. Infinite worlds exist within Him. How can we be God?"

The Guru replied, "Take my water bowl to the Jamuna River and fill it with water."

The disciple left, and in a few minutes returned with the water bowl. The Guru looked in the bowl and said, "I told you to get water from the Jamuna River. This cannot be the water of the Jamuna River."

"Oh, yes, Guruji," said the disciple. "This is the water of the Jamuna River."

"But there are fish in the Jamuna River, and there are no fish in this water," the Guru said. "There are turtles in the Jamuna River, and there are no turtles in this water. There are cows standing in the Jamuna River, and there are no cows in this water. There are people bathing in the Jamuna River, and there are no bathers in this water. How can this be the water of the Jamuna River? Go and get the water of the Jamuna River."

The disciple replied, "But this is just a small amount of water. How could it contain all those things?"

"What you say is true," the Guru said. "Now take this water and pour it back into the Jamuna River."

The disciple went to the river, poured the water into it, and returned.

"Don't all those things exist in that water now?" the Guru asked. "The individual soul is like the water in the bowl. It is one with God, but it exists in a limited form, and therefore it seems to be different from God. When you poured the water from the bowl into the river, that water once again contained fish, turtles, cows, and everything else that the river contains. In the same way, when you see your own inner Self through meditation and knowledge, you will realize that you are That and that you pervade everywhere, just like God. Then you will also be filled with all of God's powers."

We Are All God

Q: Do you consider yourself God?

SM: Yes, and I also consider you God. A great being named Siddharudha taught me Vedanta. He used to constantly repeat *Shivo'ham,* which means "I am Shiva." Once someone asked him, "Do you call yourself Shiva?"

"Absolutely," he said.

"How can you do that?" the person asked.

Siddharudha answered, "Because of your particular understanding and knowledge, you do not consider yourself Shiva. Because of my particular understanding and knowledge, I do."

In the same way, if anyone were to ask me, "Are you God?" because of my understanding I would say, "Not only does God exist within me, but He exists in every pore of my body, from head to toe. He is my entire being." When I perceive the pure Self within me, why shouldn't I consider myself God? A drop of water falls as rain on the top of a mountain. Many drops become a stream, and the stream flows down the mountain and becomes a river. The river flows until it merges into the ocean. When the river merges into the ocean, what is the original drop of water going to call itself? Is it going to consider itself a drop of rain, or is it going to consider itself the ocean?

The Shrine of a Donkey

Sheikh Nasrudin's father was the custodian of a large *dargah,* the burial shrine of a great being. Many dervishes used to worship there. Nasrudin grew up listening to their stories, and he came to feel a great desire to know the Truth. Although his father wanted him to stay at home and take care of the shrine, Nasrudin begged him for permission to go out into the world in search of God. Finally his father relented. He gave him a donkey, and Nasrudin set off. For years he wandered from forest to forest, from mosque to mosque, from shrine to shrine. When a person is deluded, he keeps wandering in his delusion. The great saint Nanakdev expressed it very beautifully: "Why do you look for Him from one forest to another? He is everywhere. He lives inside you, so why do you look for Him somewhere else?"

Nasrudin continued to wander, until one day his donkey collapsed. Nasrudin and his donkey had been great friends for a long time, and they had been traveling together for many years. So when the donkey died, Nasrudin was very sad. He threw himself on the ground and began to beat his head, crying, "Alas, my donkey is dead! My friend has left me!"

As he lay there weeping, people passed by and saw his pitiful condition. Some of them placed leaves and branches over the donkey. Others covered the animal with mud. Finally they made a shrine. Nasrudin just sat there, brooding. When passersby saw him sitting in front of the burial mound, they thought that he was a disciple worshipping at the burial shrine of some great being. So they offered flowers and money at the shrine. Soon many people were worshipping there. Many priests began to come. Incense sellers, fruit sellers, and florists began to gather outside, selling things for people to offer at the shrine. The crowds grew bigger and bigger. As more and more people made offerings at the shrine, it became very wealthy. Soon a huge mosque was built, and one thousand people began to live around it. News spread that if a person prayed at the shrine all his wishes would be fulfilled. Nasrudin began to forget his sadness. Of course, he had not attained God, but he had become very famous.

Eventually the news of the shrine reached Nasrudin's village. When Nasrudin's father heard about it, he decided to go on a pilgrimage to see the big dervish who was in attendance there. When he arrived, he was impressed by the size of the shrine. He tied his donkey to a tree outside and asked to see the dervish. Amazingly, it was his son, Nasrudin. He was extremely pleased. He embraced Nasrudin with great joy and said, "Nasrudin, you have become so famous! It is wonderful that your fame is increasing like this. But who is the great being buried here?"

"O father, what can I tell you?" Nasrudin said. "This is the shrine of the donkey you gave me!"

"Isn't that strange," exclaimed Nasrudin's father. "That is exactly how it happened with me! My shrine is also that of a donkey!"

The fact is, worshipping without the awareness of the Self is like worshipping at Nasrudin's donkey shrine.

Enlightenment Belongs to You

Q: Can I achieve enlightenment?

SM: Enlightenment is already yours. You just have to understand it. You have already realized God. You just don't have the awareness that God is within you. You assume that you are far from God. But think about this: If you don't have God right now but try to attain Him through *sadhana,* spiritual practice, there is always the chance you might lose Him again. For example, suppose I do not have a necklace. I make an effort and get one, but since the necklace is not a part of me, I might lose it after a while. In the same way, if you did not have God already, then even if you attained Him you might lose Him in the future. This is a question of understanding. You have already realized God; however, you are not aware of it.

Q: Can I become aware?

SM: That awareness is what you have to attain. It is just as if you had ten dollars in your pocket but forgot that it was there and said that you had no money. Then you put your hand in your pocket and said, "Oh, I found the money." What would you mean when you said that you had found the money? It was already there. You found what you already had.

How do we try to find God? Do we look for God as He is, or do we look for God as we want Him to be? Do we look for God as He is, or as our mind tells us He is? Do we look for a *sadhana* that will solve our problems, or do we look for problems in our *sadhana*?

I will tell you a story about my great friend Sheikh Nasrudin. Once Nasrudin got very drunk and came home late at night. He began walking back and forth outside. His wife woke up and called, "Who is it?"

Nasrudin said, "It's me."

"Why are you wandering around outside?" she asked. "Don't you have a key?"

"I have the key," he said. "My problem is that the door has no lock!"

Is this what we are doing? Are we looking for God according to our ideas, or are we looking for God as He is?

Q: Is it necessary to give up something to find God?

SM: If you truly have something, then it is necessary for you to give it up. But what do you have that you can say is yours? Your life is a gift of God. Whatever you see in this world is created by God. So what do you have that really belongs to you? I will give you a simple example. My clock belongs to the trustees of the ashram. Should I throw it away and say to God, "O God, I gave up my clock"? That would not be true renunciation, because I would be renouncing something that is not mine. In the same way, you do not have anything that you can give up. Whatever you have belongs to someone else. Not even your body belongs to you. It is a combination of the semen and the ovum of your parents.

The truth is that God is not found through any action, technique, or path. God is found through right understanding. It is because people lack understanding that they become deluded and suffer. So if you really want to renounce something, then renounce the understanding that this body belongs to you. Renounce your ego and your pride. If you cannot renounce your ego, then at least put it to good use. Instead of saying "I am a man," start saying "I am God." That is a very good kind of ego.

There is a being inside you who knows everything. Try to understand Him. He is God. Because He exists, you exist. Before a picture can be painted, there must be a canvas. God is the canvas on which your picture is painted. Do you follow?

Q: Almost. But when I asked about giving something up, I didn't mean anything material. I live by trying to understand the world rationally. My real question was, "Do I have to give up this striving to understand the world in rational terms in order to achieve God?"

SM: Just give up your wrong understanding, nothing else.

Q: Can I do this?

SM: It is you who have this wrong understanding, so certainly you can discard it. We ask the wrong questions. We try to get rid of things we don't have. We look for that which we already possess.

I can tell you that God is within every one of us, whether we understand Him or not. Why don't we experience Him? Our eyes can look at other objects, but they cannot look at themselves. In the same way, it is very difficult to see God because God is the seer of everything.

Do you understand my words? God is not an object of knowledge; He is the one who knows. Kashmir Shaivism says that one cannot attain God merely by performing different spiritual practices.[17] Techniques cannot reveal Him. Can a flashlight illumine the sun when it is the sun that lights everything?

Once Sheikh Nasrudin woke up early in the morning, before it was light. He called his disciple, Mahmud, and said, "Go outside and see if the sun has risen." Mahmud went out and came back inside.

"It's pitch black," he said. "I cannot see the sun at all."

At this, Nasrudin became very angry. "You fool!" he shouted. "Haven't you got the sense to use a flashlight?"

That is exactly what we do. To expect a spiritual technique to reveal the indwelling God is like expecting a flashlight to illumine the sun. A flashlight cannot shine beside the sun. Like the sun, the Self is always shining with its own effulgence. What *sadhana* can illumine that Self? Only through a subtle and sublime intellect can we know it. We meditate and perform spiritual practices only in order to make the intellect pure enough to reflect the effulgence of the Self.

Sit very quietly in your chair; then turn within and try to see who watches your thoughts from inside. If you keep watching in that way, you will come to know the Self. You are looking for what you have never lost. How can you attain what you already have? The Self is already working inside you; through what action are you going to find it? You will find the Self when you understand the Self. As you keep contemplating the Self, as you keep trying to understand the Self, it will reveal itself to you. So turn within. Look for that inner knower. God is in your heart. You lost Him in your heart. You will find Him only in your heart.

Notes

1. See *Bruhad-aranyaka Upanishad,* IV. 1–5.
2. *Shiva Sutras,* I.1: *Chaitanyam ātmā* — "The Self is Consciousness."
3. See Shankaracharya, *Atmabodha,* v. 36: *Nityashuddhavimuktaikam-akhandānandamadvayam/satyam jnānamanantam yatparam brahmāhameva tat* — "I am truly that supreme Brahman, which is eternal, stainless, and free; which is one, indivisible, and nondual; and which is of the nature of bliss, truth, knowledge, and infinity."
4. See *Chandogya Upanishad,* VI.12.1–3.
5. See *Kena Upanishad,* I.1: *Esho'ntāryami* — "That is the inner controller"; *Mandukya Upanishad,* v. 6: *Esha sarveshvaraha, esha sarvajna* — "That is the Lord of all, That is the controller of all"; *Bruhad-aranyaka Upanishad,* III.7.3–20.

6. *Kena Upanishad,* I.5–9.
7. *Mandukya Upanishad: Ayamātmā brahma* — "The Self is Brahman." Also see *Kena Upanishad,* I.5 – 9; Shankaracharya, *Vivekachudamani,* v. 257.
8. See Shankaracharya, *Vivekachudamani,* v. 465: *Sadghanam chidghanam nityamānanda ghanamakriyam / ekamevādvādvayam brahma neha nānāsti kinchana* — "There is only one Brahman, the one without a second, the essence of existence, consciousness, and eternal bliss."
9. See *Svacchandatantra: Nashivam vidyate kvachit* —"Nothing exists which is not Shiva."
10. See Shankaracharya, *Vivekachudamani,* v. 257: *Bhrāntikalpitajagatkalāshrayam svāshrayam cha sadasadvilakshanam / nishkalam niruparmānavaddhi yad brahma tatvamasi bhāvayātmani* — "That which is the substratum of the universe; . . . which itself has no other support; which is distinct from gross and subtle; . . . that Brahman art thou."
11. *Bhagavad Gita,* XIII.24.
12. See Shankaracharya, *Vivekachudamani,* v. 133: *Jnātā mano'hamkritivikriyānām* — "The Self is the knower of the modifications of the mind."
13. *Katha Upanishad,* II.1.4: *Svapnāntam jāgaritāntam cobhau yenānupshyati mahāntam vibhum ātmānam matvā dhīro na shochati* — "That by which one perceives both dream state and waking state, having known That as the great, omnipresent Self, the wise man does not grieve"; Shankaracharya, *Vivekachudamani,* v. 126: *Yo vijānāti sakalam jāgratsvapnasushuptishu / buddhitadvrittisadbhāvamabhāvamahamityayam* — "Which knows everything that happens in the waking state, in dream, and in deep sleep, which is aware of the presence and absence of the mind and its functions: This is That."
14. Yoga Vasishtha. Also see *Katha Upanishad,* II.1.3: *Yena rūpam rasam gandham shabdān sparshām cha maithunān etanaiva vijānāti, kim atra parisis yate etad vai tat* — "That by which one perceives form, taste, smell, sounds, and touches of love, by that alone one perceives. What is there which remains unknown to it? This, verily, is That."
15. See Kshemaraja, *Parapraveshika.*
16. *Bhagavad Gita,* XIII.14.
17. See Abhinavagupta, *Tantrasara: Upāya jālam nashivam prakashayed*—"No means of *sadhana* can reveal Shiva. Can a clay pot illuminate the conscious sun?"

THE MIND

One's own thought is one's world.
What a person thinks
  is what he becomes —
That is the eternal mystery.
If the mind dwells
  within the supreme Self,
One enjoys undying happiness.

— Maitri Upanishad

Our Worst Enemy, Our Greatest Friend

There is one great obstacle that keeps us from knowing the Self, and that is the mind. The mind veils the inner Self and hides it from us. It makes us feel that God is far away and that happiness must be found outside. Yet the same mind that separates us from the Self also helps us to reunite with it. That is why the ancient sages, who were true psychologists, concluded that the mind is the source of both bondage and liberation, the source of both sorrow and joy, our worst enemy as well as our greatest friend. That is why, if there is anything worth knowing in this world, it is the mind.

The sages of the Upanishads said that the mind is the body of the Self.[1] The Self shines through the mind and makes it function. But although the Self is so close to the mind, the mind does not know it. The mind is always moving outside, focusing on external objects, and as a result it has become very dull. It has lost the capacity to reflect the radiance of the Self, just as a lake whose waters are filled with silt loses its capacity to reflect the sun. However, when we practice meditation, the mind goes deeper and deeper within, and becomes more and more quiet. When it is truly still, we begin to drink the nectar of the Self. That is why yoga and meditation came into existence: to quiet the mind, to make it free of thoughts, and to enable it to touch its own source.

The Value of the Mind

Before we can meditate successfully, we have to understand the mind. The mind is infinitely valuable; only because it exists can we be called human beings. My Guru used to say, "If someone loses his hand, he can still live. If someone loses his leg, he can still live. If someone loses his eyes, he can still live a very good life. However, if someone has lost his mind, he is as good as dead."

Once a very great industrialist was brought to my Guru on a stretcher. He owned factories in which 700,000 people worked for their livelihood, but he had lost the use of his mind and was no longer conscious of what was happening around him. He needed a secretary, two doctors, and two nurses to take care of him. When Nityananda saw him he said, "If the mind is gone, everything is gone. This man was the support of so many people, but because he has lost his mind, he cannot even support his own body."

No matter how much wealth a person has, if he has not received the blessings of his own mind, his wealth is of no use to him. No matter how many skills a person has, if his mind is gone, his skills have no value. Even if his body is very strong and healthy, even if his senses of perception and organs of action function perfectly, if his mind is not well, his life does not work. A person may have a very young and beautiful body, but if his mind is sick, he is older than the most aged person. On the other hand, his body may be very old, his outer circumstances may be terrible, his family life may be falling apart, but if his mind is strong and quiet, neither unhappiness nor grief can touch him. That is why, if someone were to ask me, "What is the most important possession in this world?" I would say, "A good mind."

In India there have been many great psychologists and psychiatrists but very few mental hospitals. This is because in India people give great importance to the mind. The ancient Indian sages and philosophers did a great deal of research into the inner worlds and composed many great scriptures and philosophical works. In all these lengthy texts, very little is written about God. Instead it is the mind — the different means for purifying and stilling it — which is discussed. The sages discovered that the purer the mind is, the happier one feels. The minds of children are not stable, but they are very pure, and for this reason children are happier than most adults. However, the greatest happiness comes when one stills the mind. Most people have no idea that this is so. Instead, day and night, they let the mind run free. They let it think and brood, and in this way they make themselves agitated and restless. They believe that if the mind were to become still it would become dull, but this is not the case. A turbulent mind, a spinning, restless mind, is weak. A weak person is constantly fidgeting, but a strong person is still and calm. In the same way, a strong mind is a still mind; such a mind can accomplish anything. In fact, beings who pursued *sadhana* and made their minds quiet became so supremely happy that even if they possessed nothing, their joy remained. You can see this for yourself. Just for a few moments make your mind still, and then you will experience a joy you can experience in no other way.

Although it is necessary to still the mind, there is no point in trying to subjugate it or still it by force. The sages say, "O man, you are trying to control the mind, but little do you realize that the mind will control you." It is useless to chase after the mind, trying to quiet it forcibly, because then we merely become more agitated and troubled. But if we understand the mind's true nature, it will become still on its own.

A Ray of the Self

What is the nature of the mind? The mind is neither a material substance nor an object, but a pulsation of the radiance of the Self. The mind is nothing but a contracted form of Consciousness, the same Consciousness which has created the universe.

The *Pratyabhijnahridayam* says, *Chitireva chetana padādavarudhā chetya sankochinī chittam*[2] — "When Chiti, universal Consciousness, descends from its lofty state as pure Consciousness, it becomes *chitta,* the mind." It is the nature of Consciousness to create, and even when it limits itself to become the mind, it does not lose its true nature. Just as in the outer world the universal Consciousness creates infinite universes, when it contracts to become the mind, it creates infinite universes inside. If we look at the mind, we will see that at every moment it is giving rise to new inner worlds of thoughts and fantasies, sustaining them for a while and then dissolving them. This process goes on and on; even while we sleep, the mind keeps creating worlds of dreams. The mind is irrepressible because it is nothing but the pure energy of Consciousness.

Matruka Shakti

The basis of all the worlds that Consciousness creates inside us is the letters of the alphabet.[3] Letters and words create our thoughts, and thoughts create our feelings — our happiness and unhappiness, our depression and elation, our desire, love, pride, expectation, and jealousy. You can experience for yourself the power of letters. If you sit very quietly, you will notice how letters and words continually arise within. Suppose that you suddenly think, "I am a fool." Letters have come together to form words, the words have formed a sentence, the sentence has a meaning, and the meaning creates an effect. When that thought crosses your mind, you feel pain. Then suppose that you think, "I am beautiful." As soon as that thought crosses your mind, you feel happiness. That is how the letters create your inner state.

According to the sages of Kashmir Shaivism, the power that gives rise to all these letters and words is called *matruka shakti,* the power inherent in the letters of the alphabet. The Sanskrit word *matruka* means "letters." *Matruka shakti* is a form of the universal Consciousness, and it is this power which is responsible for all the agitation of the mind. Day and night, it works within us, creating innumerable worlds of thoughts and feelings. Day and night, the individual consciousness moves among these inner worlds, experiencing pain and pleasure.

The *matruka shakti* is the source of our sense of individuality and separateness. One of the aphorisms of the *Shiva Sutras* explains this: *Jnānā dhisthānam mātrukā*[4] — "It is the power of sound inherent in the alphabet that is the source of limited knowledge." Because of the ideas created by the activities of *matruka shakti,* we have come to consider ourselves imperfect individual beings rather than the all-pervasive Self; we have come to see duality in the universe instead of realizing our oneness; we have become performers of limited actions rather than experiencing our omnipotence. Yet when it is understood, the same *matruka shakti* that limits our awareness can also help to expand it. Just as our thoughts can weaken us and make us small, they can also make us stronger and take us closer to the Self. If we keep thinking of ourselves as miserable, insignificant, and weak, we remain bound. But if we consider ourselves and the entire universe to be pure Consciousness, if we continually think of ourselves as the Self and repeat the mantra of the Self, then we are using the *matruka shakti* to help us experience our true nature.

By understanding the workings of the *matruka shakti,* we can liberate ourselves from it very easily. Most people confuse the changes taking place in the mind with the Self, and that is why they are led here and there by the mind. But one who understands the play of the *matruka shakti* knows that when his mind is agitated, it is not he himself who is agitated. He realizes that all the turbulence in the mind is merely the play of *matruka.* He identifies himself with the inner observer, the witness of the agitation, and simply watches from a distance the endless activities of the *matruka.* He makes his mind steady and turns his bad thoughts into good thoughts. With the help of the awakened Kundalini, his mind turns within and becomes still. And then the Self reveals itself to him on its own.

The Therapy of the Sages

Q: How can meditation help the therapist?
SM: True psychology is born of meditation. The scriptures of meditation are the greatest works of psychology. Psychology is not just talking, talking, talking. Real psychology is yoga. There was a great sage called Maharshi Patanjali whose *Yoga Sutras* are the authoritative text on yoga. Patanjali said that through yoga one can still the movements of the mind. That is true psychology. One cannot cure the troubles of the mind by talking, nor can one steady the mind by using herbs or

drugs. Drugs may calm the mind for a while, but once the effect of the drugs fades away, the mind will return to its former state. One can straighten out the mind only by making it still, by calming the thoughts and feelings that cause it to become agitated. If psychotherapists truly understood what the mind is and improved their own minds with meditation, they would be able to practice great therapy.

Q: When you speak about meditation for therapists, do you also mean that therapists might be able to teach meditation?

SM: They can teach meditation, and by meditating themselves they can also become better therapists. Then they can very easily help other people still their minds.

Q: Many people have spoken of the difference between psychotherapy, in which one brings up feelings such as anger and hostility, and the Eastern disciplines, in which one stills the mind and quiets those feelings. Would you comment on that?

SM: Eastern philosophy says that one should purify and strengthen one's mind. It does not say that one should repress one's feelings. If feelings come up and you let them go, it is fine. As long as you don't become caught in your feelings, as long as you don't act on them, no harm will be done. But it is even better if you can eliminate your negative feelings through right understanding.

Western psychology says that one should express one's feelings. But if a person feels like committing suicide, what are you going to tell him? Will you tell him to go ahead and commit suicide, or will you tell him to control himself?

I heard a story about a psychologist who used to teach his patients not to repress their feelings. Once at an important conference he was lecturing on the necessity of giving vent to one's feelings. During the psychologist's talk, a patient who happened to be at the conference ran up to him, caught hold of his beard, and slapped his face. People grabbed the patient and tried to force him away from the psychologist. "Why are you stopping me?" he asked. "I was just letting out my feelings!"

Because they practice therapy with this kind of attitude, many people are destroying themselves. If you keep letting your feelings out and acting on them, they will never stop arising. Look at your own mind. Has it ever been satisfied with one thought? Look at your own life. Have your desires ever been satisfied by your acting on them? Desires and emotions are endless. If you satisfy one, another arises.

If you tell people to express their feelings, how will you save them? Eventually they will certainly act on them, because actions are performed as a result of feelings. If instead of merely encouraging people to express their feelings you teach them to control the mind through yoga, then they will no longer act blindly. In our yoga scriptures the mind is represented as the horse that pulls a chariot. The reins are in your hands. If you let the horse go anywhere it wishes, it will take you into a pit. You should not be defeated by your own mind. You should still the mind, purify the mind, discipline the mind. You should bring it under control with your intellect.

Q: Many people come to psychotherapy who felt profoundly unloved as little children. How can they overcome these early feelings?

SM: From now on, they should start loving themselves. There is no point in their trying to remember that they were unloved as children.

When I was studying Vedanta, I had a friend who later became a swami. Whenever we talked about our parents, I would speak of mine with great pride. I would tell him how well they had taken care of me, and what great presents they had given me, and how beautifully they had fed me. When I talked like that, my friend would get angry and complain that his parents had done nothing for him, that they had given him nothing. One day I asked him, "How much land did you have, and how large was your family?"

He replied, "We had no land. My father was dead, and my mother earned a few pennies doing menial work. She had a hard time making enough money to feed me, and I had to be taken care of by another family."

"You fool!" I said. "You've been blaming your parents for not giving you what they didn't have. My family was very wealthy, and they could give me everything because they had everything. But when your parents had nothing, how could they give you anything?"

Just as my friend's parents had no money, many parents have no love. Parents can take very good care of their children, and they should. They can feed them, teach them, send them to school, discipline them, and try to give them everything, including love. But if they do not have any love in their hearts, how can they give love to their children? Similarly, if a child himself does not have love inside, if he cannot imbibe love, how can he derive any love from his parents? Today it is the custom for people to keep saying "I love you." But can a person really obtain any love from hearing those words? Only when a person turns within and becomes immersed in his own inner Self can he truly experience love. Therefore, people should look for love within themselves. No one can obtain happiness from others.

Q: I hesitate to ask patients who are severely depressed or psychotic to meditate, because I am concerned about them becoming absorbed in their depression. Is meditation for everyone?

SM: If you explain to such people what meditation is, if you teach them meditation, they will meditate with great success, and meditation will help them. Sometimes people with weak minds come to our ashrams, and through meditation they improve.

The Power of a Thought

Once there was a temple in a town called Vishnupuri. It was the custom for each of the trustees of the temple to put a gold coin in the donation box every month. As one of the trustees watched this go on month after month, his mind became a little twisted. He kept thinking, "Just once, I'll put in a copper coin. Nobody will find out." So one month he put a copper coin in the box. But at the end of the month, when the trustees opened the box, they discovered that there were no gold coins inside—only copper ones. Everyone else had put in copper coins, too.

Thought has immense power. One person who always thinks good thoughts can make a hundred people think good thoughts. However, if one person always thinks bad thoughts, he can make a thousand people think just like him. This is the power of the mind.

The Holy Man and the Prostitute

In a certain town in India lived a *sadhu.* He was very well respected, and among his disciples were many kings, artists, scientists, and other important people. This *sadhu* maintained very strict rules of purity. He ate neither meat nor fish. He stayed away from garlic and onions. He neither drank nor smoked. He prayed three times a day. He always appeared to be repeating the mantra with his eyes closed, opening them only when he had to see someone.

The *sadhu* lived on the first floor of his building, and on the same floor in the opposite building lived a prostitute. Every day the prostitute practiced her profession, singing and dancing and doing all the things that prostitutes do. And although the *sadhu* was celibate and physically pure, he was obsessed with her.

He would watch her constantly, thinking, "Hey, that's the second fellow who has gone to her today. Now there's a third. There goes a fourth. Look, she's hugging him!" All day long, he watched the prostitute, thinking how wicked and sinful she was. "Why does a pure being like me have to live across the street from a wretched prostitute?" he would wonder.

But when the prostitute had some spare time, she would look toward the *sadhu* and be filled with remorse. She would think, "What a pure and holy being he is. And look at me—what a bad state I'm in. Alas, alas! There is no hope for me."

Many years went by like this, and one day both of them died. The *sadhu* died surrounded by his disciples, and his funeral rites were performed with great honor. Precious materials were put on his body; sandalwood and incense were burned. The prostitute, however, died alone, and nobody knew of her death until the body started to stink. Finally, the city officials came and sprinkled DDT in the house. Then they dragged the body out and buried it without any ceremony.

The souls of the *sadhu* and the prostitute went to the next world to be examined at the passport office of *dharma*, righteousness. Their files were checked, and both of them were given slips of paper indicating where they were to go. The prostitute's slip of paper said "heaven" and the *sadhu's* paper said "hell."

The *sadhu* was terribly upset. He cried, "What kind of justice is this? You send a wretched prostitute to heaven and a pure person like me to hell! How do you explain this?"

The passport official said, "Come this way." He pulled out the files and showed them to the *sadhu*. "It is true that you kept your body very pure, that you performed many religious rites and rituals," he explained. "That is why, when you died, your body was treated with the highest respect and buried with the greatest honors. But this is an account of what you thought about. Day after day, you kept thinking, 'She is a wretched creature. She is so wicked. Look at all those men who are coming to her.' "

Then the passport official pulled out the prostitute's file. "This is what she thought about," he said. "Every day she said to herself, 'O *sadhu*, you are so pure and sublime. O *sadhu*, holy man, save me. Deliver me.' Of course, her body performed impure actions, and as a result it was treated disrespectfully and given a pauper's burial. But because her thoughts were high and pure, she has been sent to heaven, and because you thought about sin and wickedness, you have to go to hell."

Like the *sadhu*, we have become our own enemy; we are not willing to think good thoughts for even half an hour. We have not developed the knack of thinking well of others. We keep asking, "What defect does he have? What fault does she have?" We have never learned to find out about people's purity or about their good qualities. We forget that by thinking negatively of others we are creating an entire world of negativity for ourselves. All our thoughts leave their traces in our psyche. Whatever thoughts we direct at others, whether negative or positive, actually have their strongest effect on us. Every thought is like a seed cast in the mind, the fruits of which we ourselves will receive later on. Prahlad, a great devotee of God, said to his father, "O father, know that whatever harm a person thinks of inflicting on others, whatever harmful acts he commits in thought or deed, leave impressions imbedded in his own mind. Henceforth, they will cause him suffering, sorrow, and anxiety." Therefore, let only good thoughts move in your mind.

Sitting Under the Wish-Fulfilling Tree

There was once an unfortunate man who kept roaming from one place to another. In the course of his wanderings he came to a forest. He sat under a tree and felt himself becoming very calm. A gentle breeze was blowing, and as he looked around, the man saw that the forest he was sitting in was beautiful.

"If I only had a companion," he thought, "I would be completely happy." The tree he was sitting under happened to be a wish-fulfilling tree. A wish-fulfilling tree is divine, and it is said that if anyone sitting under it makes a wish, that wish is instantly fulfilled. So at that very moment a beautiful girl appeared. The man was enraptured.

She sat down next to him, and for a while he was content. But then he thought, "It's a pity that the two of us have to sit under a tree, exposed to the elements. It would be much better if we had a house with a few bedrooms and a dining room equipped with all the amenities. Then I would lack nothing." Immediately, the house he had wished for appeared.

Delighted, he went into the house with his sweetheart, sat down, and had a loving chat with her. Then he said, "Look, what's the point of living like paupers in this house? I'd like to live like a lord. If we only had a butler and a couple of servants to serve us food." In the twinkling of an eye, a butler and two servants appeared.

The man called the servants over and said, "Prepare us two delectable dishes." Before long, the butler brought two servers containing gourmet food. The man tasted the food and it was delicious. But then he began to wonder, "What's going on? I wished for a wife, and she appeared and cuddled me. Then I wished for a house and got a beautiful house. Then I wished for a butler and two servants and they appeared. Then I wished for delectable dishes and they, too, materialized. What's happening? There must be a demon here!"

A demon immediately appeared in front of him, with his mouth wide open. "Oh, no, he'll eat me up!" the man cried. Of course, the demon devoured him, and that was the end.

This wretched fellow trapped himself in his imagination. At first he thought of good things, but in the process of imagining them, he also imagined a demon and his own death. If, instead of imagining a demon, he had thought, "God must be giving me all these things," his fate would have been different. If he had just wished to become an enlightened person, a great Siddha, he would have attained something. But instead he imagined his death and in that way brought it about.

This is all there is to the world we live in. In the heart is the wish-fulfilling tree of divine Consciousness, and we are seated right in its shade. We keep creating our own worlds of thought and imagination. We think, "I am a sinner," "I am inferior," "I am this," and "I am that." We get trapped in our own webs, and then one day we die.

A great sage described the world as he saw it: "There is no world, there are no men, there are no women, there is no sin, and there is no illusion. What we see is nothing but the supreme play of cosmic Consciousness." This is how we, too, should see things. We should think of ourselves as Consciousness. We should think of ourselves as the Self.

The Mind in the Realized State

Q: What is the role of the mind in the realized state, and what is the experience of the mind in that state? Do ideas continue to come up?

SM: Even after one attains Self-realization, the mind remains alive. The mind will never cease to exist, although its quality may change. When the mind is outgoing and moves among external objects, it becomes contracted. It is enveloped by impurities and becomes worldly. In the state of Self-realization, the outgoing tendency of the mind lessens. Instead of moving outside, the mind turns within. When it tends outward and moves among worldly objects, it takes the form of those objects. In the same way, when it turns within, it merges in the Self and takes the form of the Self. Realization is nothing but the merging of the mind in the Self. In the scriptures, this state is called the death of the mind, but actually the mind doesn't die. It dissolves in the Self and becomes one with it. The mind's quality of mindness still exists, but it is not different from Consciousness.

As long as the physical body continues to exist and we have to live in this world, the mind helps us to carry out our mundane functions. However, in the realized state, its nature is different. It doesn't function as a mere mind; it functions with all the power of Consciousness. It becomes stable and free of thoughts; it becomes still. Unhappiness is nothing but the net of thoughts, and when we go beyond thoughts, we experience supreme bliss. Moreover, as the mind becomes one with the Self, it acquires the power of the Self. Then it is able to do a lot of work. It can even transmit Shakti through a thought.

Notes

1. See *Bruhad-aranyaka Upanishad,* III.7.20: *Yo manasi tishthan manaso'ntaraha, yam mano na veda, yasya manaha sharīram, yo mano'ntaro yamayati, esha ta ātmāntaryāmy amrutah*—"He who dwells in the mind, yet is within the mind, whom the mind does not know, whose body the mind is, who controls the mind from within, He is your Self, the inner controller, the immortal."
2. Kshemaraja, *Pratyabhijnahridayam,* v. 5.
3. See *Tantrasadbhava: Yā sā tu mātrukā devi paratejahsamanvitā / tayā vyāptamidam vishvam sabrahmabhuvanāntakam* — "O Goddess, the universe right from Brahma down to the earth is pervaded by *matruka,* who is full of the luster of the supreme 'I'-consciousness."
4. *Shiva Sutras,* I.4.

THE INNER POWER

Contemplate Kundalini,
Who is supreme Consciousness,
Who plays from the base of the spine
 to the crown of the head,
Who shines like a flash of lightning,
Who is as fine
 as the fiber of a lotus stalk,
Who has the brilliant radiance
 of countless suns,
Who is a shaft of light as cool
 as hundreds of nectarean moonbeams.

— Shri Vidya Antar Yaga

The Power of the Self

If we truly want to deal with the problems of the mind, we must turn within and awaken our own inner power. Then the mind will come easily under our control, and very naturally we will experience the Self. It is said that the Self is attained through knowledge. Yet the knowledge that reveals the Self is not the worldly knowledge we acquire from books or schools. It is the inner understanding of unity, the realization that we and the Absolute are one and the same. How do we obtain this knowledge? It comes to us spontaneously when our inner energy awakens and unfolds within us.

This inner energy is known as Kundalini, and it exists within every human being. It is more subtle than our breath, and this is why we are not ordinarily aware of it. The Kundalini is spoken of in nearly every tradition, though it is known by different names. In China it is called Chi. In Japan it is known as Ki. The scriptures of Christianity call it the Holy Spirit. In India it has many names, but it is known mainly as Shakti, cosmic energy. Shakti is the dynamic aspect of the formless and attributeless supreme Absolute; the sages of India worship Her as the great goddess, the mother of the universe. Shakti is the divine creative energy, the force through which the Absolute brings everything into existence.

Another name for Kundalini is Chiti, universal Consciousness. The *Pratyabhijnahridayam,* one of the principal scriptures of Kashmir Shaivism, describes it in an aphorism: *Chiti svatantrā vishva siddhi hetuhu*[1]—"Universal Consciousness creates this universe in total freedom." Moreover, it creates the universe out of its own being, using no outside material.[2] Consciousness becomes every particle of this material world, manifesting as all the forms and shapes we see around us. It pervades everything in the visible and invisible universe and carries out infinite functions. Yet in its power and purity it remains completely untouched.

This mighty power is the power of our own Self. The same Shakti that creates the entire external universe also pervades the human body from head to toe and in this form is called Kundalini. Kundalini is the vital energy that makes everything in the body work. It enables us to see through the eyes, hear through the ears, smell through the nose, and experience touch through the skin. The power of Kundalini makes the heart beat, the blood flow, and the breath come in and go out of the body. This is the external aspect of Kundalini, which supports our lives.

However, Kundalini also has an inner, spiritual aspect, which ordinarily lies dormant. According to the yogic scriptures, this inner Kundalini resides specifically at the center of the body, in the *muladhara chakra,* a subtle energy center at the base of the spine. When it is awakened, our spiritual journey truly begins. Just as the external aspect of Kundalini allows us to function in the outer universe, the inner Kundalini allows us to function in the internal world.

In our present state, our awareness flows outward. Because of the limitations of the mind and senses, we think of ourselves as the body and identify with the experiences of our senses. We do not know the all-pervasiveness of Consciousness or our own divinity. Once the Kundalini is awakened and begins to work within us, our mind and senses turn inward, and we begin to experience our true nature. The *Pratyabhijnahridayam* says, *Balalābhe vishvam atmasāt karoti*[3]—"When one acquires the strength of Kundalini, one is able to assimilate the entire universe into oneself." One no longer remains a limited, bound creature; one comes to know, by direct experience, one's true glory.

The Awakening

There are many ways in which Kundalini can be awakened. It can be aroused through intense yogic practices such as physical exercises, breathing techniques, and mantra repetition. Or it can be awakened through chanting and intense love for God. But there are dangers in awakening the Kundalini by these means, either because of the intensity with which the practices must be performed, or because once it is awakened, the power has no direct guidance. The only safe and sure way of awakening the Kundalini is *shaktipat,* the process by which a Siddha Guru, a perfected master, transmits a spark of his own fully unfolded power directly into a disciple, activating the dormant Kundalini and setting it into full operation.

Shaktipat is the secret initiation of the greatest sages, and it has been passed down from Guru to disciple since before recorded time. It is not the monopoly of the Indian tradition. Great beings of every tradition had their inner energy awakened and could awaken it in others. Some spoke of it specifically, while others used veiled terms. If Jesus moved his hand over someone, that person would be transformed, and great love and joy would arise in him. That was nothing else but *shaktipat.* Saint Francis, too, had this power. And it was through *shaktipat* that Ramakrishna Paramahamsa gave his disciple Swami Vivekananda an instantaneous experience of the Absolute.

A Guru can transmit Shakti to a seeker in four ways. One is by touch. Through the grace of his own Guru and through intense practice, a true Guru has completely unfolded his Kundalini energy so that it fills every pore and blood cell of his body. Shakti continually flows from him and passes into whomever he touches. The Guru can also give formal initiation through a word (a mantra), a look, or even a thought. However, a Siddha Guru does not have to give deliberate initiation in order for a seeker to receive his Shakti. The Shakti that saturates his being also pervades the atmosphere around him, including the things he has used or worn. A person who is receptive simply has to come near the Guru to receive Shakti, just as he might catch the germs of a cold from someone who has a cold. It was like this with my Guru. He seldom gave formal initiation. But so much Shakti flowed out of him that people received *shaktipat* even from his abusive words. Sometimes he would ask someone to leave, and that person would linger. Then my Guru would raise his arm and throw a towel or some other object at him, shouting, "Go now!" At that instant, the person's Shakti would be awakened. A Guru can also authorize a disciple to give *shaktipat,* and the Shakti transmitted in this fashion is the same as the Shakti of the Guru. In fact, a person can receive *shaktipat* even if he is thousands of miles from the Guru.

The Effects of Shaktipat

Although the same Shakti is given to everyone, people's capacities are not the same. Therefore, when the Shakti is awakened, it manifests differently within different people. Once, when I had a cold, a homeopathic doctor gave me some medicine. "Take it once and you will be all right," he said. I followed his instructions, and my cold was cured immediately. Because I had recovered so quickly, I told the doctor that I would like to recommend the medicine to others. He said, "No, you can't give it to anybody else."

"Why not?" I asked. "It worked for me."

"Your body is not like other people's bodies," he said. "It won't work in the same way for others."

I had been practicing yoga for many years and my body was very pure, so I imbibed the medicine fully. Similarly, the intensity with which someone receives *shaktipat* depends on his mental state, on the practices he has performed, on his faith and his desire to receive the Shakti, and on his past actions and the accumulation of his sins and virtues. In some people, the Shakti works immediately and with great intensity; in others, it may take some time to manifest and may work less intensely. The scriptures say that there are twenty-seven degrees of intensity with which a person can receive *shaktipat,* depending on his capacity to hold the Shakti.

When a very qualified person receives *shaktipat,* he will have an immediate experience of his all-pervasiveness. However, most people do not have the strength to bear such an experience immediately. For some, the awakening brings visions of vibrant inner lights. Others experience intense bliss. Others feel extreme mental agitation. Some people feel an aching sensation throughout the body. Some feel indifferent or become depressed. Some people feel intoxicating love. Some have experiences of extraordinary physical energy. Once an Australian businessman came to our Indian ashram and received *shaktipat* while sitting in the meditation room. His body was filled with so much energy that he went running through the ashram grounds, leaping over six-foot walls and moving so fast that no one could catch him.

There are also some people who at first feel nothing at all. But these people need not worry, because sooner or later they will experience the awakened Shakti. Once a woman from France came to our ashram. She stayed for eight days. At the end of that time, she came to me and told me that she had not had any experiences of the Shakti and was going to leave. "Very good," I said to her. That day she left for France. No sooner had she boarded the airplane, than the Shakti grabbed her and she went into a state of meditation. Once a person has received Shakti, it will always stay with him, no matter where he goes, and sooner or later it will begin to work.

Siddha Yoga

The process that begins once the Kundalini is activated by a Guru is known as Siddha Yoga (the perfect yoga) or Maha Yoga (the great yoga). Siddha Yoga is the path of the perfect masters, the means by which all the greatest saints and sages attained perfection. The lineage of these Siddha masters has existed since the beginning of creation, and its power has been handed down from Guru to disciple in an unbroken lineage.

Siddha Yoga is completely self-propelled. Like a machine that operates automatically once it has been started, the process of Siddha Yoga continues without pause once it has been set in motion. After the Shakti is activated, yoga happens spontaneously within. One does not have to make an effort to practice yoga; it goes on all the time, during the course of one's daily activities. Whether one is working in an office or factory, carrying out one's business, or taking care of one's children, the Shakti keeps unfolding within. That is why, once the Kundalini has been awakened, a seeker does not have to perform strenuous spiritual practices. The Shakti itself gives every individual the experiences that are necessary for him.

All the classical yogas take place spontaneously in a seeker whose Shakti is awakened. For this reason, it is said that Siddha Yoga encompasses all other yogas. For example, yogic postures, locks, and breathing techniques may occur spontaneously during meditation. Sometimes the body may shake and sway. All of these movements, known as *kriyas,* are manifestations of hatha yoga. They take place in order to purify all the channels in the body, because unless these channels are clear, the Shakti cannot work with full force.

The specific postures and movements that occur in an individual are precisely the ones he needs for the purification of his system. This is one of the things that makes Siddha Yoga so significant. When we practice hatha yoga on our own, we often do not know which exercises our body actually needs, and so we may practice postures that are unnecessary or even harmful to us. But when hatha yoga occurs spontaneously through the action of the Kundalini, we automatically perform whatever postures are appropriate for us.

Just as hatha yoga occurs after the Kundalini is awakened, other yogas take place spontaneously as we need them. Love wells up within, as in bhakti yoga. Knowledge of the Self begins to arise on its own, as in jnana yoga. We start to work selflessly in the world, as in karma yoga. Addictions disappear, and we begin to develop positive qualities such as patience, self-control, discipline, and compassion. We no longer have to make a great effort to meditate; instead, meditation occurs spontaneously. In meditation we may see inner lights or visions or hear inner sounds, as in laya yoga. We develop great interest in chanting, repeating the name of God, and reading the scriptures, as in mantra yoga. Ultimately, when the Kundalini rises to the topmost spiritual center, the *sahasrara,* we attain the *samadhi* state, the state of equality-awareness. This is the manifestation of raja yoga, which culminates in the realization of God within.

The Worldly Journey

As Kundalini works within us, it automatically transforms our outer life as well as our inner state. Our outlook changes, and we begin to see everything around us through new eyes. Relationships that may have seemed painful or dry become joyful and filled with affection. We feel an ever-expanding love for our family and friends, and gradually we start to see everyone around us as different forms of our own Self. Ordinary activities and tasks, which might have been boring to us, begin to take on new savor. Kundalini is a great source of motivation and inspiration. It makes a writer a better writer, a doctor a better doctor, a statesman a better statesman, a businessman a better businessman, a mother a better mother. All talents and skills lie in its womb, and when Kundalini is awakened these abilities manifest in our lives. Kundalini improves whatever needs improvement; where we have imperfections, it strengthens and balances us.

It is said that worldly pleasure and spiritual perfection can never be found together. But this is not the case when we follow the path of Kundalini. A scripture says, "Where there is liberation, there are no enjoyments, and where there are enjoyments, there is no liberation. But when one walks on the path of the supremely beautiful Kundalini, liberation and worldly enjoyments go hand in hand." This world, after all, is Kundalini's creation; it is Kundalini itself. So it should not be surprising that Kundalini is able to take care of every aspect of our lives.

The Central Channel

The outer changes in our lives are only an indication of the real work of the Kundalini. It is inside us that Kundalini creates its miracle. The human organism contains 720 million *nadis,* or channels. Some carry blood, some carry nourishment, and some carry *prana,* the vital force. Of these *nadis,* the *sushumna nadi* is paramount. Also known as the central channel, the *sushumna* is located in the subtle body in the area corresponding to the physical spinal column, extending from the seat of the dormant Kundalini at the base of the spine to the topmost spiritual center in the crown of the head. The *sushumna* is the support of our whole psychophysical system, regulating the functions of all the *nadis.* The entire journey of our spiritual evolution takes place within it. The *Shiva Sutras* say, *Madhya vikāsāt chidānanda lābhāha*[4]—"When the central channel is unfolded, one experiences the bliss of Consciousness."

Usually we speak of the dormant Kundalini Shakti as residing at the mouth of the *sushumna,* at the base of the spine. But actually there are three different types of Kundalini within the body, each of which exists in a different location. One is known as Prana Kundalini, one is known as Chit Kundalini, and one is known as Para Kundalini. Although Kundalini can be awakened at any of these locations, it is usually activated at the base of the spine.

After one receives *shaktipat,* Kundalini enters the *sushumna nadi.* The *sushumna* opens up and begins to unfold, and Kundalini moves upward, piercing the six *chakras,* or spiritual centers, that lie in its path. Then the Kundalini Shakti, which is the seed of the universe, unites with the *prana* and moves through the entire subtle and physical system, purifying all of the channels and making the body strong and fit for *sadhana,* spiritual practice. Physical diseases, as well as such negative qualities as anger, lethargy, envy, and greed, are caused by impurities blocking the flow of *prana* in the *nadis.* Once the *nadis* are purified and the *prana* can run smoothly through the body, the body is rejuvenated and the mind becomes pure.

While this purification process is taking place, latent mental tendencies are often brought to the surface. The *sushumna nadi* is a storehouse for all the impressions of countless lifetimes. In its lower region lie such feelings as lust, greed, anger, insecurity, and inferiority, while in its upper region are such qualities as peace, happiness, and knowledge. As the Kundalini travels up the *sushumna,* it expels all the negative impressions and feelings. As they arise, we experience them. For example, if your mind has a tendency to become agitated, your agitation may seem to be worse for a while. If you have a tendency to be fearful, you may feel more fear for a while. But you should not be afraid of these feelings; the Kundalini is simply working to expel them from your system. As a result, your mind will be purified and these tendencies will leave you forever.

The activated Kundalini also expels latent physical diseases. That is why, if you have a latent illness, you may be sick for a short time after Kundalini awakening. This does not mean that something has gone wrong. Kundalini is an all-knowing, all-powerful force, and it knows exactly how to work within your system.

However, it is important to take care of the inner Shakti. Once it has been awakened by the Guru, you should practice meditation regularly, repeat the mantra given by the Guru, lead a disciplined life, and in that way enhance your inner power. This should not be difficult, because once the Kundalini begins working, you will naturally find yourself becoming interested in spiritual practice. Discipline and regularity will come into your life automatically. You will develop an interest in repeating the mantra and in meditating, and as you do these practices, the Shakti of the Guru's grace will make them bear fruit for you very quickly. It is said that the work of the inner Shakti and the power of one's own effort are the two wings of the bird which carries you toward the goal. As you continue your *sadhana,* the Shakti itself will show you which practices you need. This is the greatness of the yoga that arises through *shaktipat.* It is never artificial or forced. No disciplines or techniques are imposed on you from outside. Because everything that takes place during the course of Siddha Yoga *sadhana* arises from the inspiration of the inner Shakti, it is your own; it is always appropriate for you.

The Heart Center

As the Kundalini rises up the *sushumna,* you will have innumerable experiences in meditation. There is a great spiritual center in the heart, and when Kundalini begins to work there, wave upon wave of bliss will arise. You will begin to experience the inner planes, and you will come to know why the sages have said that the inner world is much greater than the outer world. You may see future events and hear far-distant things, and other supernormal powers may come to you quite naturally. But none of these things have much importance, and you should not get trapped in them. These experiences are not the goal of the inner journey, but merely signposts along the way. Moreover, not everyone will have all of them. But anyone who meditates systematically will certainly have some of them.

Purification of the Senses

During its journey up the *sushumna*, Kundalini pierces and purifies all the sense organs, and they begin to take on divine powers. As the sense of sight is purified, you will begin to see faraway objects, and in time will acquire the capacity to see the universe as it is: a shimmering mass of blue light. As Kundalini works on the other sense organs, you will begin to hear inner celestial harmonies, to feel thrills of love throughout the body, to smell divine inner fragrances, and to taste delicious inner nectars.

The Sahasrara

Finally, after purifying all the centers, Kundalini will reach the *sahasrara* in the crown of the head, and there it will begin to play. Then bliss will throb in every pore of your body, and you will experience union with God.

The *sahasrara* is an extraordinary center, and within its vast spaces lies the tiny, sparkling blue light known as the blue pearl. This beautiful, fascinating blue light is infinitely valuable, for it is the form of the inner Self. The great saint Tukaram Maharaj described it in one of his poems: "The Lord of the universe erects a house the size of a sesame seed and lives within it." Although the blue pearl appears to be tiny, it is a seed containing the entire universe. It is extremely subtle and moves like lightning; sometimes in meditation it can be seen coming in and going out of the eyes. The blue pearl is the very life of an individual being; it is the vehicle in which the soul leaves the body after death and travels to different planes.

To see this light, to make it steady, and to enter into it, you will have to meditate for a long time. But you can be certain that if you keep meditating, through the grace of the

Kundalini, you will eventually experience it. Once your inner Shakti has been awakened by a Siddha Guru and you have begun to walk on the path of Kundalini, you are bound to reach the goal. One day, as you meditate on the blue pearl, its radiance will expand infinitely, and you will know that you pervade the universe. You will know your own divine reality, and then joy will never leave you.

The Beauty Within

Once the great saint Ramanuja went to a fair, and there he saw something astonishing. One of the greatest wrestlers of the town was walking behind a young prostitute, holding an umbrella over her, fanning her, and looking after her very attentively. Ramanuja watched for a while, and then he called the wrestler over. "You are such a distinguished wrestler," he said, "and yet you are going about holding an umbrella over a prostitute and fanning her. You are so obsessed with her that even though the sun is pouring down like fire, you do not seem to be affected by it. What is the secret of this infatuation?"

"Sir," said the wrestler, "I am attracted to the beauty of this woman's form. I am so fascinated by it that unless I see her, I do not feel satisfied. That is why I am pursuing her."

"What if I were to show you even greater beauty?" asked Ramanuja. "What would you do then?"

"I would leave her," said the wrestler.

"Then sit down," said Ramanuja. He touched the wrestler on the head and heart region and told him to sit for meditation. As soon as he received the saint's touch, the wrestler became lost in meditation and had a vision of the glorious and effulgent beauty within himself. After he got up from meditation, he told the woman to go back to her parents, and soon after he became one of Ramanuja's disciples. He had realized that the beauty inside him was greater than any outer beauty.

This is the effect of *shaktipat.* It can give us such a profound, immediate experience, that our understanding is completely changed, and we acquire great interest in the Self.

In Scientific Terms

Q: Can the process of Kundalini awakening be understood in scientific terms, and is it valuable to try to understand the process, not as a substitute for the experience, but as a way of furthering it?

SM: It is very difficult to explain it in what are called scientific terms; only the external, physical aspects of the Kundalini awakening can be described in that way. The effects of the awakened Kundalini on the body organs, the nervous system, the heart rate, and the metabolic rate can be studied with scientific instruments. But the inner, subtle aspects cannot be detected by any instruments because Kundalini is an extremely subtle force; it is pure light. For true understanding, a scientist should have his Kundalini awakened and experience it himself, and then perhaps he will be able to describe it in the terms he is accustomed to.

Many psychologists and others who are involved in Kundalini research have asked me, "How can we get other people involved?" Each person wants to get others interested in Kundalini awakening in his own way. A scientist wants to interest people through scientific discussions or investigations, while a yogi wants to interest them through yoga. Since I have been in America, thousands of people have experienced Kundalini awakening. I can describe it only in the terms that I know. You scientists should have a direct experience, and then you can describe it in your terms.

Where science ends, *shaktipat* begins. But someday even scientific researchers will recommend *shaktipat.*

How to Receive Shakti

Q: To whom does the Guru give *shaktipat?*

SM: The Guru gives *shaktipat* to a seeker who is willing to receive it. He does not decide that he is going to give it to one and not another. This is like asking who the sun gives its heat to. Anyone can tell you that a person who takes the trouble to go outside and stand in the sun will receive its heat, whereas if he stays in his house he won't receive it. The sun has no favorites. Such an idea has no meaning for the sun.

Anyone who has the Self within him — and who does not? — can receive *shaktipat.*

If you open yourself to the Guru, his Shakti will flow into you. Even if he does not give it to you, you can draw it from him by force. In the *Mahabharata* there is the story of a Guru named Dronacharya, who was the greatest master of archery the world has ever produced. He taught only princes. One day a tribal boy named Eklavya approached him and asked for lessons in archery. The Guru said, "How dare you come to me? I teach only princes, and you are a primitive boy. I won't have anything to do with you." Eklavya was not discouraged. He looked at the teacher from head to foot, evoked him in his heart, and offered him his love. Then he went back to his hut, fashioned a statue of Dronacharya, and began to worship it. Every day he followed the same routine. He meditated on his Guru's image and then practiced with his bow and arrow. After some time all his Guru's knowledge of archery passed into him through the clay statue.

One day when Eklavya was practicing archery, he saw a dog and shot an arrow between his teeth. The arrow did not hurt the dog; it just hung between his teeth. The dog had come from the ashram where all the princes were learning archery from Dronacharya, and he ran howling back. When the Guru saw the arrow in the dog's teeth, he was astonished. "I have never taught this secret to anyone," he said. "Who could have learned it?" Great teachers sometimes keep the innermost secrets of their skills to themselves. Dronacharya had communicated all the secrets of his archery to his students except this single shot. He called his royal students and commanded them to go to the forest to look for the archer. The students did as their master told them, and at last they came upon Eklavya, who was sitting in meditation before his Guru's statue. They brought him out of meditation and asked, "Who shot the arrow that is hanging between the teeth of our dog?"

"I did."

"Who taught you?"

"I learned from my Guru."

"Who is your Guru?"

"Dronacharya."

The royal princes were green with envy. They thought, "Our teacher said he taught us everything, but there is one trick he secretly taught to this student." They took Eklavya to Dronacharya and told him, "Here is the one who shot the arrow. He says that you taught him that secret, and it is quite obvious that you have kept it from us." Dronacharya asked Eklavya, "From whom did you learn this secret?"

"You refused to teach me, so I went home and made a clay image of you," said Eklavya. "I meditated regularly before it, and I made myself aware of my identity with you. Then, spontaneously, this secret revealed itself within me."

So the Guru does not have to decide to give *shaktipat.* You can compel him to give it to you as Eklavya did. Love and devotion have tremendous power. Through them you can get whatever you want from the Guru.

A person receives *shaktipat* from the Guru according to his attitude. If his attitude is very good, I do not have to give him *shaktipat*; he draws it to himself. Some people receive Shakti just by reading one of my books and only later come to find out who I am. The higher a person's attitude, the sooner he receives Shakti.

After the Awakening

Q: Is the experience of *shaktipat* ever too powerful for someone to handle?

SM: No. It is true that sometimes the experiences are strong, but the Shakti is not an uncontrolled force. When the Shakti is awakened by Guru's grace, that grace will make sure that the Shakti works in the most appropriate way. However, if a person tries to awaken the Shakti solely through his own efforts, he may have some difficulty.

Many kinds of experiences occur after the awakening of Kundalini. Sometimes, if this awakening occurs without the help of a Guru, either spontaneously or as a result of yogic practice, a person may not know what is happening to him, and he may become frightened. He may feel that his experiences are symptoms of a physical or mental disease—for example, he may mistake inner lights and sounds for hallucinations. Sometimes, after the awakening of Kundalini, a person may feel tired, dull, agitated, angry, or emotionally upset. Or he may experience insomnia, feel indifferent or negative toward himself and others, or even feel as if he were going crazy. Not realizing that such feelings are temporary and part of a process of purification which will ultimately remove all negative tendencies, some people look for methods of "curing" themselves and often become miserable as a result. Sometimes they take drugs or undergo treatments that are detrimental both physically and spiritually. That is why it is better to have one's Kundalini awakened by a master whose own Kundalini is fully unfolded. Through his grace such a being knows how to channel and guide the awakened force, and make sure that nothing goes wrong.

Q: Once we receive *shaktipat,* do we have to worry about keeping it?

SM: To hold the Shakti within you, to sustain grace, you have to live a pure life. Suppose that you are penniless and starving and, by someone's grace, you receive three dollars. You take the three dollars and go shopping. The first object you see is a harmonica. You don't need it, but driven by a whim you spend one dollar on it. Then you see a balloon. That strikes your fancy, so you buy it too. You see some other object and buy that. In this way, you have spent the three dollars and your pocket is empty. What you really need is food, but you have no money left. Similarly, you should not dissipate the Guru's grace. If you wish to conserve it, you must be very conscious and careful. Every day you should think about how to make it grow. Talk less, speak the truth, and work to earn the bread you eat. All these things will help you sustain grace.

Q: You often speak of the power of Shakti. What restrains the selfish nature from misusing this power?

SM: Can ego control Shakti? Ego will never be able to hold Shakti in its hands. Instead, Shakti will devour ego. Shakti destroys the stupidity of stupid people. It sharpens the minds of dull people. Shakti is meant to develop one's understanding and capacity for inner contemplation, to refine one's intelligence, and to help one merge in the supreme Truth. As Shakti unfolds, more and more ego will be dissolved.

The Right Motivation

Q: What is the proper motivation for someone who wishes to receive *shaktipat?* Should it be to liberate himself or to help liberate others?
SM: To begin with, a person should want to receive *shaktipat* for himself and to make the Shakti grow. Once he has become fully endowed with that divine energy, he can think about giving it to others. Only if you have something yourself can you give it to someone else. Only if you have become perfect, can you give Shakti to others. So first increase your own power.

Notes

1. Kshemaraja, *Pratyabhijnahridayam,* v. 1.
2. Ibid., v. 2.
3. Ibid., v. 15.
4. Ibid., v. 17.

THE MANTRA

Just by repeating the Name,
that which cannot be understood
will be understood.
Just by repeating the Name,
that which cannot be seen
will be seen.

— Jnaneshwar

The Mystery of Mantra

Mantra is the root of everything we do in this world. It is the basis of all our practical dealings as well as of yoga, meditation, and knowledge. Mantra is one of the most important factors in Siddha Yoga. Through the mantra, the Guru's Shakti enters the disciple, and by repeating the mantra we make that Shakti work with great force.

Mantra is sound, and sound is reverberating in everything in this universe. When water flows, it makes a gurgling sound. That is mantra. When wind blows through the trees, it makes a rustling sound. That is mantra. When we walk on the earth, our footsteps produce sound, and that too is mantra. Within human beings as well, there is a self-born, indestructible sound which repeats itself constantly, along with our breathing.

Sound has enormous power; in fact, it has the power to create an entire universe. It is written that God originally manifested as sound.[1] The Upanishads say that in the beginning there was sound, which reverberated as *Om,* and from that sound everything came into existence.[2] Even modern scientists are beginning to recognize, as our ancient sages did, that there is a vibration which reverberates ceaselessly throughout the cosmos. That vibration underlies all matter and is the substratum of everything. Just as it pulsates within all the objects in the universe, it also pulsates within us. That inner pulsation, which we can discover throbbing at the root of the mind, is the true mantra, and it is in fact nothing but

Kundalini, the divine energy. From that inner pulsation, through the *matruka shakti,* infinite letters and syllables arise, which give rise to all the inner and outer worlds.[3]

The Name and Its Object

When letters and syllables come together, they form words. Both our spiritual life and our mundane life are possible only because of words; without language, we could not carry out any of our activities. Each word we use has its own power and produces its own reaction. For example, when we go into a grocery store and ask for an apple, we are given an apple, and not anything else. This is the power of an ordinary word, which we can call a mundane mantra. Just as a mundane word puts us in touch with the object that is its goal, a spiritual mantra puts us in touch with the highest goal of human life, the Self.

Such a mantra is no ordinary combination of letters and syllables, but a living force. The name of God is not different from God. An aphorism in Kashmir Shaivism says, *Mantra maheshwaraha*—"Mantra is the supreme Lord." Mantra has been called the sound-body of God: It is God in the form of sound. In the *Bhagavad Gita* Lord Krishna says, *Yajnā nām japayajnosmi*[4]—"Among rituals, I am the ritual of mantra repetition." By this He means that while other techniques are means of attaining Him, mantra is His very being. That is why it is so easy to experience God by repeating the mantra. Mantra repetition bears fruit very quickly; the great saint Tukaram said, "With the name of God on your lips, the bliss of liberation is right in your hand."

This is not surprising when we consider how quickly even ordinary words affect us. Once a saint was giving a lecture on the power of mantra. He was saying, "Mantra has the power to take us to God." As soon as he heard this, a skeptic in the audience stood up and shouted, "That's nonsense! How can repeating a word take us to God? If we keep repeating 'bread, bread, bread,' will that manifest bread?"

The saint snapped, "Sit down, you bastard!" The man began to tremble and his face turned red. "How dare you speak to me like that?" he cried. "You call yourself a holy man and yet you go around insulting others! What kind of person are you?"

"Sir, I am very sorry if I offended you," the saint said. "But tell me, what are you feeling at this moment?"

"Can't you tell what I'm feeling?" the man shouted. "I'm outraged!"

"Oh, sir," said the saint, "I used just one abusive word, and it had such a powerful effect on you! When this is the case, why shouldn't the name of God have the power to change you?"

Like an abusive word, the mantra has its own power. However, if we want to obtain the full fruit of the mantra, we have to repeat it with full awareness of its meaning. The poet-saint Tulasidas said, "Everyone repeats the name of Rama, including cheats, thieves, and priests. But the way in which the great devotees repeated the name was entirely different, because the name redeemed them." How did these great beings realize the power of the name? The answer is found in an aphorism of Kashmir Shaivism which explains that only when we understand that the repeater of the mantra, the syllables of the mantra, and the object of the mantra are one will the mantra show its results quickly.[5]

Most of the time, we repeat the mantra with the wrong understanding, thinking that the syllables of the mantra and the object of the mantra are different from each other and from ourselves. That is why the mantra does not bear immediate fruit for us. If you think about this, you will understand that the same thing is true on a mundane level. Suppose that someone calls you an idiot. If you do not accept the word "idiot" as referring to you, you will not react to it. But if you identify with it, you may become so angry that your blood heats up. If you were to identify yourself with the name of God as easily as you identify yourself with an abusive term, you would experience its effects at once.

The Influence of Mantra

The mantra can completely transform our inner being. Our inner state is created by the thoughts and feelings that continually arise in us. Outwardly we may appear to have fixed identities—one person may appear to be a lawyer, another an engineer, another a doctor, another a professor. But inside, we are a continually changing mass of consciousness. When we project the beam of mantra into this fluctuating mass, it stabilizes it and focuses it in one direction, the direction of the Self. The sages have said that only the mantra can help us transcend our confusion, our fantasies, and the constant changes of the mind.

Moreover, as we repeat the mantra, it begins to permeate all the constituents of the body. Whatever thought or feeling arises in the mind has an immediate effect on the body; even doctors now recognize that our thoughts can make us sick or help to cure us. Our thoughts pass from the mind to the *prana,* from the *prana* into the bloodstream, and through the bloodstream to the entire body. The name of God flows through our system in the same way, removing all the toxins from the blood, purifying the *prana,* freeing the mind from negative emotions, and making joy arise in the heart.

As the influence of God's name penetrates the mind, the mind itself becomes the name;[6] in other words, the mind becomes divine. Repetition of the name of God causes a kind of earthquake in our inner consciousness. Whatever thoughts arise in our daily life are recorded within us and form impressions that are difficult to remove. But when we repeat the name, all these thoughts and impressions are erased, and the name of God is recorded. At every moment, what we think is what we become. If the face of anger arises in the mind and we identify ourselves with it, we become filled with anger. In the same way, if we continually repeat the mantra with great love and interest, we will become absorbed in God. By its very nature the mantra has the ability to transform our awareness of ourselves as individuals into an awareness of ourselves as God.

We should not regard mantra repetition as a mere technique. A great saint said that before realization mantra repetition is a spiritual practice but that after realization it becomes the purest nectar. That is why the greatest saints went on repeating God's name even after attaining liberation. To them, mantra repetition was not a mere practice; it was itself the attainment.

The Conscious Mantra

There are 70 million mantras which can be found in books or obtained from different teachers. However, if a seeker wants a mantra that will transform him, he must obtain a live mantra, one that is imbued with the power of Consciousness. There are two types of mantra—the *chaitanya,* or conscious, mantra and the *jada,* or inert, mantra. An inert mantra is found in a book or received from a teacher who has not realized its power. Such a mantra has no strength; it is merely a dry and ineffective collection of letters. But a *chaitanya* mantra is obtained from a Guru who himself received it from his own Guru and who, by fully unfolding its power, has attained Self-realization. Behind it is the full force of the Guru's realization, and it starts its work within a seeker immediately. As the disciple repeats the mantra, his dormant Shakti is awakened, and a new life is created within him.

It is said that a person has two fathers: the father of the body, who gives him life through his semen, and the spiritual father, the Guru, who gives him life through the mantra. Just as the body born of semen is nourished by food, so the body born of mantra is nourished by the repetition of mantra. Therefore, let your life become filled with mantra. Repeat it continually, no matter what you are doing. If you repeat it when you are going to sleep, you will have a very deep sleep. If you repeat it when you wake up, you will spend your day happily. Mingle the mantra with all your activities. Repeat the mantra when you wash your face. Repeat it when you eat your breakfast. Repeat the mantra while you travel to your office, and repeat it on the way home. Repeat the mantra while you bathe, and repeat it when you drink your tea. Anyone who is addicted to smoking will check his pocket before he leaves home to make sure that he has his cigarettes. In the same way, you should become so hopelessly addicted to the mantra that you are always certain you are carrying it in your heart.

It is said, *Mananāt trāyate iti mantraha*— "Mantra is that which protects the one who repeats it." The power of the mantra is beyond your imagination. You can understand the meaning of the mantra, but you cannot know its potency. You can contemplate the mantra, but you cannot measure its strength. Mantra is the living force of God. Therefore, repeat it with respect. If you devote even a half hour or an hour every day to repeating the mantra, you will function much more effectively in your worldly life, and your heart will be filled with joy. Your Shakti will unfold very quickly, so that soon you will begin to experience the Self.

The Science of Sound

The science of mantra is very great, because mantra is the ladder by which we reach the formless Consciousness. According to the mantra scriptures, speech manifests within a human being on four levels. Most people associate speech with its grossest level only, the level of articulated speech known as *vaikhari.* Yet the truth is that the tongue does not speak by itself; the gross sound arises from a subtler level, *madhyama,* which is experienced in the throat. Beneath this subtle level is a still deeper level called *pashyanti,* the causal level of speech, which is experienced in the heart. But the origin of sound lies still deeper, in the transcendental level of speech, which is experienced in the navel region and is called *paravani.*

Let us examine how words arise. By the time words reach the tip of the tongue, they have taken a gross form. However, before they make their way to the tongue, they have passed through all the levels of speech. The subtlest level of speech is *paravani.* This is the region of pure, unmanifest sound, where there is neither duality nor nonduality. *Paravani* is actually all-pervasive. It is the subtle vibration from which the entire universe, with all its forms, is born. Here all sounds, all words, and all language arise from pure Consciousness. Just as a peacock egg contains all the colors of a peacock's feathers in a potential form, all syllables and words exist within *paravani* in an undifferentiated seed form. As sound arises, it passes to the third level of speech, *pashyanti.* At this level, through the work of the *matruka shakti,* it begins the process of assuming form, but it is not yet in a completely differentiated state.

When sound passes from this level to the *madhyama* level of speech in the throat, it assumes a recognizable form. It is at this point that words begin to create the world of differences inside us. Here words are fully formed, although they have not yet been uttered. Finally, they pass to the gross tongue, the *vaikhari* level of speech, where they are articulated and can be heard.

The Descent of the Mantra

The mantra has the power to penetrate through these gross and subtle levels of sound, erasing our sense of difference and carrying us back to its source. When we repeat it, it passes from the gross to the subtler levels, until it reaches the pure Consciousness from which it has arisen.

In the initial stage, we repeat the mantra silently on the level of the tongue, listening to the mantra as we repeat it and focusing the mind on the tip of the tongue, where the mantra is vibrating. After we have repeated the mantra on this level of speech for a while, it goes deeper, to the *madhyama* level in the throat. One repetition at this level is equal to thousands of repetitions with the physical tongue.

From the throat center the mantra descends to the *pashyanti* level in the heart, where its vibrations become even more powerful. One repetition in this center is equal to thousands of repetitions in the throat center. When mantra repetition is taking place at the *pashyanti* level, we feel wave upon wave of bliss and we acquire unusual powers; we are able to see and hear what is distant and to know the past and the future. Now the repetition of the mantra goes on continually, and we remain in an intoxicated state. Finally the mantra passes from the heart center to the navel center, the *paravani* level of speech, where it touches the Self. Then the entire body becomes permeated by the mantra, and we experience the supreme Truth. This is how the power of the mantra is realized.

Once a being has realized the potency of the mantra, once he has made it touch the Self, the power of the Self pervades his words and makes them unfailing in their effect. That is why the mantras of Siddha yogis inevitably bear fruit. One who has fully realized the mantra obtains all the powers of the Self. Any word that comes from his mouth comes from *paravani,* the space of Consciousness. For this reason, every word he utters is a mantra and will always do its work.

The Great Redeeming Mantra

In Siddha Yoga, we give two mantras. One is *Om Namah Shivaya,* and the other is *So'ham.* The goal of both mantras is the same; only the method of repeating them differs.

Om Namah Shivaya is known as the great redeeming mantra and as *panchakshari,* the five-syllable mantra.* It means "I bow to Shiva." Shiva is the supreme reality, the inner Self. Shiva is the Consciousness that dwells in all.

The mantra that the Guru imparts to a seeker is the mantra he received from his own Guru. This is known traditionally as the Guru mantra or initiation mantra. *Om Namah Shivaya* is the initiation mantra of the Siddhas, the lineage of perfected masters which traces its origin back to Shiva, the primordial Guru. This mantra has been handed down from Guru to disciple since the earliest times, and the entire line of Siddhas, from Shiva to my Guru, Nityananda, stands solidly behind it. Through the mantra, the Shakti of the Guru enters the disciple; this is why it is called the mantra of initiation.

Underlying this mantra is a great secret. As we chant the five syllables *Namah Shivaya,* the five elements that comprise the body are purified. Each of the syllables corresponds to one of these elements: the syllable *na* to the earth element, the syllable *ma* to the water element, the syllable *shi* to the fire element, the syllable *va* to the air element, and the syllable *ya* to the ether element. Each syllable purifies its corresponding element. As long as the body and the mind are not completely pure, we cannot fully benefit from our spiritual practice. Therefore, we repeat *Om Namah Shivaya* to help cleanse them.

**Om Namah Shivaya* is called the five-syllable mantra even though we repeat six syllables, because *Om* is not considered a syllable, but the seed of all letters.

Many of the greatest sages of ancient times repeated *Om Namah Shivaya,* and it is said that all mantras are contained in its womb. The sage Upamanyu explained its secret in this way: "If this mantra vibrates continually in your heart, then you have no need to perform austerities, to meditate, or to practice yoga. To repeat this mantra you need no rituals or ceremonies, nor must you repeat it at an auspicious time or in a particular place." This mantra is free of all restrictions. It can be repeated by anyone, young or old, rich or poor, and no matter what state a person is in, it will purify him. The sages said, "This mantra is mysterious. Repeat it, repeat it, repeat it."

In the Indian scriptures there is a story about the great sage Sananda. He was completely immersed in *Om Namah Shivaya,* and he repeated it constantly; in fact, he never spoke any other words. Finally, his end came. When a person's time comes, no matter who he is, the messengers of one world or another come to take him. The messengers of Shiva came for Sananda. As they were transporting him to the higher world, he saw a realm which was emitting black smoke and from which terrible cries were coming. He asked the messengers, "What is that place?"

"It's hell," the messengers answered.

"I want to see it," said Sananda.

"You can't," said the messengers. "You haven't repeated the right mantras."

"Either you take me there," Sananda replied, "or I will not go with you to the higher world." The messengers had no choice, so they took him to hell. When he arrived and saw all the souls burning in agony, Sananda was horrified. Whenever a person is shocked, he reveals what he has been thinking about throughout his life. When Sananda saw what was taking place in hell, he cried, *Om Namah Shivaya!* The force of his mantra repetition immediately purified all the souls in hell, and they were taken to heaven with him.

This is the power of *Om Namah Shivaya.* If you repeat it, no matter what you have done, no matter what sin you have committed, it will redeem you.

How to Repeat the Mantra

You should repeat the mantra silently, at the same speed at which you talk. You can also coordinate it with the breathing, repeating it once with the inhalation and once with the exhalation. Repeat it very carefully, just as a miser looks after his wealth. Listen to it as you repeat it, and in that way your mind will become permeated with mantra. If you repeat the mantra when you breathe in and breathe out, it will circulate throughout your body, permeating every one of your blood cells. Then even the room in which you have been repeating the mantra will become saturated with it.

In my ashram in India there used to be a special room where I lived for a long time and where I meditated and repeated the mantra. Eventually I moved into other quarters, and the room was then kept locked. Several years ago, a government official came to the ashram. He told me, "I have heard many people say that if anyone stays in your ashram, he can get into meditation very easily." I took him to the room, showed him inside, and told him to sit for meditation. "What mantra should I repeat?" he asked. "If you hear a mantra in this room, repeat that," I told him. When he came out, he said, "I heard *Om Namah Shivaya* coming from the walls! The entire room was repeating it!"

Mantra is a living force. If you repeat it one-pointedly and for a long time, it will permeate your whole environment.

The Natural Mantra

So'ham is the natural mantra, the mantra of the Self.* It does not belong to the East or the West or to any religion. *So'ham* is inherent in all of us; it repeats itself continually, along with our breathing. As long as this mantra keeps going on inside us, there is life in the body. As soon as it stops, we are no more.

**So'ham* is also known as *Hamsa* mantra. *So'ham* and *Hamsa* are the same mantra; the order of the syllables is simply reversed.

As your breath goes out and comes in, it produces two syllables. The breath goes out with the sound *so* and comes in with the sound *ham.*[7] Every time the breath goes out and comes in, one repetition of the *So'ham* mantra takes place. Whether one is an Indian or a Westerner, one repeats this mantra unconsciously thousands and thousands of times every day. The meaning of *So'ham* is "I am That." Through these two syllables, we contemplate our oneness with the supreme principle.[8]

Prana, the vital force, is not different from the supreme Consciousness. An aphorism in Kashmir Shaivism says, *Prāksamvit prāne parinatā* — "Universal Consciousness has become the *prana.*" First, Consciousness becomes the *prana* and then, through the mantra, it powers the breathing process in the human body. It is the supreme energy, Kundalini, which throbs in the form of the inhalation and exhalation, constantly uttering the syllables *ham* and *so.* This is the significance of *So'ham:* It is the divine throb of the supreme energy. *Ham,* the syllable that comes in with the inhalation, is the supreme "I"-consciousness, the perfect "I am," which is God. *So,* the syllable that goes out with the exhalation, is God's power, Shakti, which takes the form of the universe. The moment we realize that it is Kundalini which is repeating *So'ham,* we become free of all suffering. We transcend our individuality and are reestablished in our original nature.

The *Vijnana Bhairava* is one of the most important texts of Kashmir Shaivism. It is in the form of a dialogue between Bhairava, or Shiva, the supreme Lord, and Shakti, His creative power. In it, Bhairava describes 112 centering techniques (called *dharanas*) for holding the awareness of God within. The first *dharana* explains the technique for practicing *So'ham,* and it is the simplest and most beautiful of all. Bhairava says, "O Goddess, the *prana* [exhalation] goes out, and the *apana* [inhalation] comes in. At the place where they merge, one experiences the state from which creation emerges and into which it is absorbed."[9]

The source of *So'ham* is the heart. It is from the heart that the syllables arise, and in the heart that they subside. If you observe your breath, you will notice that it arises from within with the sound *so,* goes out of the body to a distance of about twelve fingers, and dissolves there. A fraction of a second later, the inhalation arises with the sound *ham* and goes back into the body. It merges in the heart for a split second and then arises again in the form of *so.* Between the inhalation and the exhalation, and between the exhalation and the inhalation, there is a fraction of a second which is absolutely still and free of thought. That space is the space of the Truth. When you breathe in and out, listening to *ham* and *so,* you should focus on that space for as long as it lasts. As you practice the technique, the space will gradually expand.

This is a natural *sadhana,* a natural yoga. It is known as *ajapa-japa,* the unrepeated mantra repetition. Since *So'ham* goes on within you all the time, you do not have to make an effort to repeat it. All you have to do is become aware of it. You do not need any faith. You just have to watch the space of the Truth.

But since this technique is very subtle, you have to practice it for a while in order to understand it. Whenever you sit quietly, follow your breath and listen to the mantra. If you do not immediately become aware that the mantra is repeating itself, you can repeat the syllables along with your breathing. In a few days you will be able to synchronize the mantra with your breath. Soon you will begin to hear the mantra naturally. If you practice it for a while, you will experience the Self.

The practice of *So'ham* is recommended in the Upanishads and the Vedas. The Shaivite sages also say that to attain the Self one should practice *So'ham.* The great being Brahmananda sang:

> O *sadhu,* contemplate the mantra *So'ham.*
> The fingers do not move on the rosary,
> The tongue does not utter the letters.
> The mantra repeats itself within.
> Watch it. . .
> Those who contemplate *So'ham* ceaselessly,
>   discarding worldly entanglements,
> Attain the supreme state, O Brahmananda.
> Their worldly bondage is destroyed.

A Matter of Understanding

Q: Repeating the *So'ham* mantra even once brings me into meditation and connection with the Self. During meditation I seem to be imposing *So'ham* on this already existing state of absolute stillness. Should I continue to repeat it even though the breath has stopped and stillness is attained? Are the goal and practice of *So'ham* the same?

SM: Yes, the goal and practice of *So'ham* are the same. *So'ham* means "I am That," and if you practice it with complete concentration, being aware of the breath coming in and going out, you will experience That. However, the truth is that you do not really have to practice it, because you are already That.

King Janaka used to go to a forest outside the city and practice his *sadhana* there. He would sit on the bank of a river and repeat *So'ham.* One day the great sage Ashtavakra was passing through the forest and noticed Janaka repeating *So'ham, So'ham*—"I am That, I am That." He thought, "My goodness! What is he up to?" No one can ever predict how a great being is going to teach something. His ways of teaching are unique. Ashtavakra sat down in front of Janaka. In one hand the sage was holding a *kamandalu,* a water bowl, and in the other a T-shaped stick called a *yogadanda,* which yogis rest their chins on while meditating. Then he began to repeat, "This is my yoga stick, this is my water bowl. This is my yoga stick, this is my water bowl."

When Janaka heard this, he opened his eyes, wondering, "Where has this nuisance come from?" Then he closed his eyes and once again began to repeat his mantra. The sage began to repeat *his* mantra even louder. "This is my yoga stick, this is my water bowl. This is my yoga stick, this is my water bowl." Again Janaka opened his eyes and looked at the sage, and again he closed them and returned to his mantra. Finally, the sage began to shout, "This is my yoga stick, this is my water bowl!"

Janaka was very disturbed. "O son of a sage," he cried, "what are you doing?"

"O Your Majesty," Ashtavakra replied, "what are *you* doing?"

"I am repeating my mantra."

"I am doing the same thing," said Ashtavakra. "I am saying 'This is my yoga stick, this is my water bowl.' "

"O brother," Janaka said, "who told you that your yoga stick and your water bowl do not belong to you? Why do you have to keep shouting about it?"

"Who told you that you aren't That?" asked Ashtavakra. "Why do you have to keep shouting about it?"

The practice of *So'ham* is a matter of understanding. Just as the yoga stick and the water bowl belonged to Ashtavakra and he did not have to say so, in the same way you do not have to keep repeating "I am That," because you are That.

Which Mantra?

Q: You give out two mantras—*Om Namah Shivaya* and *So'ham.* Should we use them alternatively or use just one all the time?

SM: If you like you can repeat *So'ham* for meditation and *Om Namah Shivaya* at other times. You have to coordinate *So'ham* with the breath, and if you really want it to be effective, you have to remain aware of the space between the breaths. This is difficult to do while you are carrying on your daily activities. Therefore, it is better for most people to use *Om Namah Shivaya* for *japa. Om Namah Shivaya* and *So'ham* have the same goal and the same power. Both come from *Om.* Both belong to the Siddha lineage. So it does not matter which you repeat. The important thing is that the mantra you repeat comes from the Guru and that you stick to that mantra. You should not take one mantra from one teacher this week and another mantra from another teacher next week and a third mantra from a third teacher the week after that. Going from one mantra to another in this way is like trying to ride two boats at one time. If you try to put your feet in two boats, you will fall in the river. You shouldn't keep changing your mantra like you change your clothes. Once you have decided on a path, you should stay with it.

Faith and Love

Q: How should we repeat the mantra?
SM: When the sage Narada asked Brahma, the creator, "What is the secret of repeating the mantra?" Brahma replied, "The secret is to repeat it with great faith and love."

Once there was a *sadhu* who lived on the bank of a river. Nearby lived a milkmaid to whom he had given the mantra. Every day, with great devotion she would bring milk to the *sadhu.* One day, during the rainy season, the river flooded. The milkmaid stood on the bank of the river, wondering how she could take the milk to her Guru. Then she remembered, "When my Guruji gave me the mantra he said, 'You can go across the ocean of existence by repeating this mantra.' And this is only a river." So she closed her eyes, repeated the mantra with great faith, and walked across the water to the other shore. The Guru was in his room. She knocked on the door and called, "Babaji, open the door! I have milk for you."

"How did you get here?" he asked.

"Don't you know? When you gave me the mantra you said that if I repeated it, I would go across the ocean. This was just a small stream."

When he heard this, the *sadhu* became swollen with pride. "What a state I must have attained if even my milkmaid can walk on water with my mantra!" he thought. A few days later, he had to go to town. Once again the river was flooded. He stood on the bank, wondering what to do. Then he remembered proudly, "Because of my mantra, the milkmaid crossed the river." He began to repeat the name, stepped into the river, and sank like a stone.

The mantra bears fruit according to our attitude. If we repeat it with faith and love, it will take us quickly to the goal. If we repeat it with a dry heart, it will be much less effective.

The Power of Chanting

Chanting is a significant and mysterious practice. It is not just a practice: Chanting is the highest nectar, a tonic that fully nourishes our inner being. If we want to experience love, the greatest means is chanting God's name. Chanting opens the heart and makes love flow within us. It releases such intoxicating inner bliss that simply through the nectar it generates we can enter the abode of the Self. Gauranga, Mirabai, Namadeva, and many other great saints attained perfection by chanting the name.

"O my mind, chant God's name," sang the great Siddha Manpuri. "Chant it day and night—only then will you find true repose. O Manpuri, by singing God's name become completely desireless and delight in the inner Self. This path is easy, but it brings the highest bliss."

Tukaram Maharaj, who was a great teacher of the divine name, wrote, "Not only the heart, but the entire being is rejuvenated by chanting." Nowadays people go to psychiatrists and psychotherapists to help them discard their negative feelings. But chanting is the greatest of all therapies for removing negativities from the heart. Jnaneshwar Maharaj said that when one chants the name of God, all the sins of this world are destroyed.[10] Not only does chanting purify us inwardly, but it also purifies the atmosphere around us, even reaching the plants, germs, and insects. Moreover, if we chant the name of God with great respect and a full heart, without expectation, we can attain God in a very short time. God lives in any place where His name is sung. In Jnaneshwar's great commentary on the *Bhagavad Gita,* Lord Krishna says, "O Arjuna, I do not dwell in the heavens, nor am I seen in the orb of the sun. I transcend even the minds of yogis. But if you ever need Me, know that you can find Me in a place where devotees are chanting My name with love."[11]

This is the greatness of chanting. It is a magnet that draws God's power; by chanting the divine name, we can have God instantly in our heart. God has two aspects. One is His pure, transcendent aspect, which is completely beyond name or form. The other is His personal aspect, which has form and qualities. The name is that personal aspect. The name is the purest elixir because it is the very form of the Lord. A person who understands the mystery of the name knows that when we chant God's name, we touch God with the tongue, and when we listen to it, we hear God through the ears. A saint said, "It is surprising that although the nectar of chanting is available to a human being, he still insists on living his life with a sad and indifferent heart and deprives himself of the love of the divine name."

The glory of chanting is immeasurable. Tukaram explained it very beautifully when he sang, "With the sweetness of my chanting, I will make the knowers of the Truth drool. I will bring great yogis out of *samadhi.* I will make pilgrims desert the holy places. As I chant, I will make my own body the embodiment of love. Through the glory of my chanting, my entire being will become the Absolute."

Notes

1. *Adau bhagawan shabd'ha rasihi.*
2. See *Chandogya Upanishad,* II.23.3: *Tān abhyatapat, tebhyo'bhitaptebhya aumkāraha samprāsravat* — "[Prajapati] brooded on [the worlds] and on them, thus brooded upon, issued forth the syllable *Om.*" Also see *Mandukya Upanishad,* I: *Om ity etad aksharam idam sarvam, tasyopavyākhyānam,bhūtam bhavad bhavishyad iti sarvam aumkāra eva yaccānyat trikālātītam tad apy aumkāra eva* — "*Om,* this syllable is all this. . . . All that is the past, the present, and the future, all this is only the syllable *Om.* And whatever else there is beyond the threefold time, that too is only the syllable *Om.*"
3. See Kshemaraja, *Shiva Sutra Vimarshini,* commentary on II.7, for an explanation of how the world arises from letters.
4. *Bhagavad Gita,* X.25.
5. An aphorism of Kashmir Shaivism says, *Pruthak mantrah pruthak mantrī na siddhyati kadāchana*—"If the mantra is recited with the idea that the mantra and its reciter are different, it will never yield perfection." A similar statement occurs in *Shrihanthi-samhita,* quoted in Kshemaraja's *Shiva Sutra Vimarshini.* Also see Kshemaraja, *Shiva Sutra Vimarshini,* commentary on II.1: "That by which one ponders inwardly oneself as being not different from the highest Lord is mantra."
6. See *Shiva Sutras,* II.1: *Chittam mantraha*—"The mind [which constantly contemplates the highest reality] is mantra."
7. See Kshemaraja, *Shiva Sutra Vimarshini,* commentary on III.27: "The breath is exhaled with the sound *sa* and inhaled again with the sound *ham.* Therefore, the empirical individual always repeats the mantra *Hamsa.*"
8. See Kshemaraja, *Shiva Sutra Vimarshini,* commentary on III.27.
9. *Vijnana Bhairava,* v. 24: *Ūrdvhe prāno hy adho jīvo visargātmā paroccharet utpattidvitayasthāne bharanād bharitā sthitihi.* Also see *Vijnana Bhairava,* 25: *Maruto'ntar bahir vāpi viyad yugmānivartanāt / Bhairavyā bhaira vasyettham bhairavi vyajyate vapuh.*
10. Jnaneshwar, *Jnaneshwari:* IX.196.
11. Ibid., IX.206–207.

MEDITATION

Like oil in sesame seeds,
  butter in cream,
  water in the river bed,
  fire in tinder,
  the Self dwells within.
Realize that Self through meditation.

— Svetashvatara Upanishad

The Natural Path

For the sake of attaining the Self, many techniques and practices have been developed. Some people perform rituals and ceremonies, but attain only fatigue. Others practice strenuous austerities, but experience only agitation. Others take up yoga, but get stuck in *pranayama* and concentration techniques. Still others devise their own techniques, claiming that they lead to the Truth, but end up being trapped in their own deceptions.

It is certain, however, that to experience the Self we must follow a spiritual practice. Even to achieve something in daily life, we have to work for it. We cannot satisfy our appetite merely by reading a description of a delicious meal. To satisfy our appetite we have to eat, and in the same way to have an authentic inner experience we have to follow an authentic *sadhana.* However, the best *sadhana* is not strenuous and difficult, but completely natural. It is one that we can do in our own world, without abandoning our family, our work, or our daily activities.

For a while during his *sadhana* Lord Buddha was performing severe austerities. One day two musicians happened to pass by the place where he was sitting. One was saying to the other, "Do not tighten the strings of your instrument too much or they will break. Do not keep them too loose or they will produce no sound at all. Follow the middle path." These words hit Lord Buddha with great force. He felt that they had been said just for him. Immediately, he gave up his severe *sadhana* and began to follow an easy and natural one.

Meditation is a natural *sadhana,* and it has been recognized by all the saints and sages as the most direct means of perceiving the Self. The *Bhagavad Gita* says, *Dhyānenātmani pashyanti*[1] — "Through meditation, the Self is seen." Meditation is universal. It is not the property of any particular religion or nationality. It does not belong to Hinduism, any more than sleep belongs to Hinduism. Is there such a thing as Hindu sleep or Christian sleep or Muslim sleep? Sleep is our own property, and in the same way meditation belongs to us. In fact, not only human beings meditate; everything in nature is in meditation. When a bird glides in the sky, it is in meditation. When an animal stalks its prey, it is in meditation. The Upanishads say that the earth holds its position through the power of its meditation, that the wind blows through the power of its meditation, and that fire burns through the power of its meditation.[2]

Meditation in Life

Meditation is not some strange technique that we have to learn with great effort and difficulty. There is already a strong element of meditation in our lives, but we are simply not aware of it. When we read, when we study, or when we do research, we have to focus the mind. When we drive a car or operate machinery, we have to pay attention. When we explain something to a friend, we have to concentrate in order to make ourselves understood, and our friend has to concentrate in order to understand us. Lovers meditate on one another. A mother meditates on her child. Whatever we accomplish in this world we accomplish through the power of concentration, which is nothing but meditation. Until now, our concentration has been focused on mundane things. But if we simply change the direction of our meditation, if we simply turn it within, we will be meditating on the Self. Just as when the mind focuses outside it perceives the outer world, when it looks within it sees the inner world. It is as simple as that.

Meditation is a complete path. It not only brings inner experiences, but removes all the worries and tensions of the mind and washes away the sins of countless lifetimes. Meditation is not merely a technique; it is a means by which we can actually see the Truth as it is. By meditating more and more on the inner Truth, we ourselves become that Truth. Through meditation our inner awareness becomes steadily deeper, and our understanding of internal and external things becomes sharper. Above all, meditation stills the wandering mind and establishes us forever in a state of peace that remains stable no matter what happens around us. Through meditation we become aware of our fundamental unity with all things. We cannot attain that awareness by reading books or listening to lectures. We can attain it only through direct experience. To have that experience we must pass from one state of awareness to another, moving gradually to deeper and deeper levels of our being. In meditation this is exactly what happens: We pass from the level in which we have the awareness "I am the body" to the level in which we have the experience "I am God."

The Object of Meditation

If you want to meditate successfully, you must first understand what it is that you are to meditate on. People meditate on all kinds of objects using many different techniques. Some meditate on their fantasies. Others meditate on certain centers of the body. But if you examine these techniques carefully, you will see that none of them can take you to the Self. If you want to reach the Self, you have to meditate on the Self. You have to meditate on the witness within. If you do not understand the witness, you will go in the wrong direction in your meditation. The truth is that when most people meditate, they do not meditate on the Self. Instead, they pursue the mind, trying to eradicate its thoughts. If a thief came into your house, you might take a stick in your hand and try to chase him away. But is this the way to meditate? What is your job in meditation? Are you supposed to chase the mind, or are you supposed to meditate on your Self? Your true relationship is not with the mind, but with the Self. Therefore, understand what the Self is. Find this out: Are you supposed to know the Self, or is the Self the knower of everything? Are you supposed to meditate on the Self, or is the Self the one who is meditating on you?

The Self is Consciousness.[3] It is self-effulgent, shining by its own light. It knows everything that goes on inside you. Therefore, it is not going to come within your grasp. The mind, intellect, and ego can operate only because some small portion of the light of Consciousness is illumining them. So how can these inner instruments show you the Self? God cannot be thought about by the mind, because it is God who sets the mind to thinking. In the *Kena Upanishad* there is a statement: *Yan manasā manute yenāhurmano matam, tadeva brahma tvam viddhi*[4]—"That which is not thought by the mind but by which the mind thinks—know that as the Absolute." It takes a very subtle intellect to grasp this, but if you understand it you will not have to make an effort to meditate. You will simply become aware of that which is meditating on you.

Suppose that during meditation, something comes up inside. First you become aware that something is there. Then you know exactly what it is. You identify it as a good thought or a bad thought, as an image or a fantasy. The one who makes you aware of the existence of that thought or image, and of exactly what it is, is nothing but the Self, the witness. Inside and outside, no matter what happens, no matter what you do, the Self sees everything. To know that knower is true meditation.

Therefore, do not try to impose any conditions on your meditation. Simply turn your attention within and meditate on the knower who is always aware. Do not worry if your mind spins. So many clouds come and go in the sky, but the sky remains pure; it is not affected by the clouds. In the same way, when thoughts arise and disperse in the mind, the Self is not disturbed by them. If you can, clear your thoughts away. If you cannot, try to perceive the witness of those thoughts. If you focus on that witness, the thoughts will calm down on their own.

When the mind becomes entirely free of thoughts, the light of the Self will naturally reveal itself. That is why the scriptures of meditation say that the true meaning of meditation is total stillness of mind.[5] However, not everyone is able to still the mind all at once, and therefore the sages have prescribed different techniques of meditation, according to people's capacities.

The Mantra

One of the greatest of all techniques is mantra repetition. Mantra and meditation are companions; the mantra is a tremendous help in meditation. The mind is accustomed to focusing on an object, and through the mantra one simply gives it the right kind of object. Just as when the mind is given an outer object to dwell on it roams in the outer world, when the mind is given the mantra it begins to dwell in the inner world.[6]

When you use the mantra during meditation, you should focus on the mantra itself and try to perceive the place where it arises; try to see where it is vibrating, and listen to it. Repeat the mantra as if it were your own name, making no distinction between the syllables of the mantra, the object of the mantra, and your Self. In this way, your mind will automatically turn inside and become focused on the Self.

The Posture

In order to meditate, you have to sit in a particular posture. The sitting posture, or *asana,* is the foundation of meditation, and it must be firm if the temple of meditation is to be sturdy. Most people associate the word *asana* with strange positions like the peacock pose or the plow posture. But these external postures are not very helpful to one who is trying to reach the Self. The real meaning of the term *asana* is a position in which one can remain still and comfortable for a long time.[7] If the body keeps moving, the mind also becomes restless. But if one keeps the body still, the mind gradually becomes still and concentrated.

The yoga texts have described many *asanas,* but for meditation only three are important. The first is *padmasana,* the lotus posture; the second is *sukhasana,* the easy posture; the third is *siddhasana,* the perfect posture. If you cannot meditate comfortably in any of these postures, then lie down in *shavasana*, the corpse position, flat on your back on the floor or on a hard mattress. The most important factor in any meditation posture is that the back be kept straight, because when the spine is straight, the mind naturally becomes centered in the heart.

Pranayama

Another vital aspect of meditation is *pranayama*, the breathing process. Many methods of *pranayama* are explained in the yogic scriptures. However, in meditation you should pursue the *pranayama* that happens on its own. Do not try to control your breath, but let it move in and out naturally. God has created both the *prana* and the movement of the *prana*, and He has done it correctly. If you repeat the mantra while sitting comfortably in a posture, the *prana* will very naturally go out and come in, in rhythm with the mantra, and be retained for a few seconds. This is natural *pranayama*. As the breathing becomes steady, the mind will become steady, and you will not have to make an effort to quiet it. As you continue to repeat the mantra in conjunction with your breathing, the *prana* will become more and more still, and you will begin to go deeper and deeper in meditation.

The Secret of Meditation

These are the four important factors in meditation: the object of meditation, which is the inner Self; the mantra, which will put you in contact with the Self; the meditation posture, which should be steady and comfortable; and the natural breathing rhythm, which will arise as you repeat the mantra. When these four factors come together, you will experience the state of meditation.

However, the real secret of meditation on the Self is *shaktipat*. If you want meditation to come easily and naturally, your inner Shakti, the Kundalini, must be awakened through the grace of a Siddha Guru. Then you will no longer have to struggle for meditation. The Shakti will center your mind in one place, and through the mantra given by the Guru your consciousness will naturally and easily be carried inward, toward the Self.

However, you must meditate regularly and persistently, going deeper and deeper within. Then meditation will be a gradual and systematic unfolding of your real inner being. Along the way, you may have many kinds of experiences, but the ultimate state is beyond all experiences. In that state there is only bliss. True meditation is to become immersed there.

The Inner Journey

As you move closer and closer to that state in meditation, you will pass through your inner bodies. Although you are ordinarily aware of only your physical body, there are actually four bodies which constitute the total human system: the physical body, the subtle body, the causal body, and the supracausal body.* In deep meditation, as the Kundalini unfolds, these bodies can be experienced directly. The physical body is the body of the waking state, in which we eat and drink and pursue the various activities of daily life. Our awareness is centered in the eyes and functions through the sense organs. When we are in the waking state, we identify with the body and all that relates to the body. If the body is experiencing pleasure, we think we are experiencing pleasure. If the body is experiencing pain, we think we are experiencing pain.

As you begin to go deep in meditation, you may find yourself surrounded by a red aura the size of your body. This red light fills all the channels of the body, and by its glow you can see all the bodily fluids circulating through the nerve channels, arteries, and veins. You can even see food being carried from one part of the body to another. The red light represents the physical body.

As you go deeper in meditation, you will pass from the physical body to the subtle body, which you will see as a thumb-sized white light. The subtle body is the vehicle in which we experience dreams. In the dream state, our awareness resides in the throat center and functions through subtle sense organs, experiencing subtle dream-pleasures and dream-

---

*The four bodies also correspond to the four levels of speech—*vaikhari, madhyama, pashyanti,* and *paravani,* which are discussed in the chapter on mantra.

pains. In this state, we do not experience the pains and pleasures of the waking state; for instance, if someone has a boil on his arm, he will be in pain during the day, but as soon as he goes to sleep, he will no longer feel the pain. When you experience the subtle body in meditation, you will become aware that you are different from the physical body.

I am not speaking theoretically about these bodies. During my own journey of meditation, I perceived them directly, just as I am describing them. If your inner Shakti is awakened and you meditate regularly and systematically, you too will experience them. Eventually you will come to the third body, the causal body, which you will see as a black light the size of a fingertip. The causal body is the body of deep, dreamless sleep, and when you are experiencing it in meditation, you will be in a state of total darkness and oblivion. In this state, the small self retires into the universal Self, and you will no longer be conscious of who or what you are. You will experience great peace, and your intellect will become centered in itself. This is called the state of the void.

The Final Attainment

Anyone who believes that the void state is the culmination of meditation will come to the end of his journey here. But if you continue to meditate with great love and with deep faith in the Guru and the Kundalini, you will go beyond the void. You will pass from the causal plane to the supracausal plane, from the body of the void state to the body of the transcendental state, which is the scintillating point of blue light known as the blue pearl.[8]

At first, you will see the blue pearl only at moments. It will move constantly, darting in and out of the eyes. However, if you are a courageous seeker, if you are very intense in your practice and have great devotion for God and your Guru, you will eventually be able to make the blue pearl stand still. Then if you are a worshipper of a particular form of God, you may one day see the form you love within the blue light. Toward the end of my *sadhana,* I had this experience in meditation. I saw the blue pearl expand until it became the size and form of a human being. The body of this Being was composed entirely of scintillating rays of Consciousness, and with great amazement I realized that I was seeing the supreme unmanifest Being I had read about in the scriptures. The Being spoke to me, blessed me, and then reduced His size and again took the form of the blue pearl. It was this experience that gave me faith in the personal form of God. Before, I had believed only in God's formless, attributeless aspect, but after I had this vision, I realized that God has the power to assume any shape. If God, who is pure Consciousness, can take form as the universe, why should He not be able to assume a human form and appear before a devotee?

However, if you have such an experience, you should not consider it the culmination of meditation. One day, after the blue pearl has remained steady for a long time, it will expand infinitely, and its light will fill the universe. Then with intense wonder, you will see that the whole world is shimmering and scintillating with this blue light. You will realize that you yourself are that light, and your feeling of smallness will vanish. Your sense of limitation will melt away, and you will realize your own vastness and your own glory. Absorbed in the intoxication of divinity, you will know only bliss and oneness. When Mansur Mastana attained this state of transcendental oneness, he said, "That place is the tavern of the ecstatic ones. It is the goal of meditation; it is the house of God." It is the country of eternal bliss, where there is no pain, no sorrow, and no death.

Once you have experienced this state, your understanding will be completely transformed. Just as in your present state you know that you are the body, once you have become established in that highest state, you will know that you are God. You will know that just as waves arise and subside in the ocean, the entire cosmos arises and subsides in the Self. Then you will no longer have to close your eyes to go into meditation, because wherever you are and whatever you are doing, you will experience the Self. You will see the same Self in every particle of the world, and whether you are eating or drinking, giving or taking, coming or going, alone or in the midst of people, you will remain immersed in that Self. This state is known as natural *samadhi,* and it is the highest level of perfection. When a person is in this state, he lives in God and moves in God. Whatever he does is worship of God. His entire being is immersed in God; his inner ecstasy remains the same in happiness or sorrow, in praise or blame, in health or illness. Such a being is called a *jivanmukta,* one who is liberated while in the body. When you reach this state, you will have fulfilled the purpose of your meditation and the purpose of your life.

Where and When to Meditate

Set aside a place for meditation—a room or a corner of a room—and purify it by chanting the mantra. Try not to let anything happen that will disturb its atmosphere. In the place where you meditate regularly, the vibrations of meditation will gather, and after a while it will become very easy to meditate there. For the same reason, you should set aside special clothes and a mat for meditation. Do not wash them often, because the Shakti will accumulate in them and make it easy for you to meditate.

If possible, meditate at the same time every day. The early hours of the morning, between 3:00 and 6:00, are best, but you can meditate at any time that is convenient. If you become accustomed to meditating at a certain hour, your body will develop the habit of meditation. If you cannot meditate at any other time, you can meditate lying down in your bed before you go to sleep at night. Then if you fall into meditation, your meditation will continue through the night.

The Method of Meditation

Sit quietly and turn your attention within. Become very still and focus on your inner being, or focus your attention on the mantra, either *Om Namah Shivaya* or *So'ham.* Let the mantra carry you within.

When a thought appears on your inner screen, do not try to wipe it away. Instead, consider every thought or fantasy to be no different from the Consciousness which is the goal of your meditation. Remember that the mind is nothing but a contracted form of Consciousness and that if it gives up its awareness of being the mind, it will merge back into Consciousness again. After all, what are the images in your mind composed of? Are they made of anything material, or are they made of Consciousness? Sugar candies can be shaped like horses, camels, or dogs, but no matter what form they take they are still made of sugar. In the same way, even though Consciousness has become innumerable thoughts, these thoughts are all made of Consciousness. If you understand this, then you will have very good meditation.

Let your awareness be in the present moment. Do not let it wander away. If you are completely present, God is also present. Lose yourself in meditation. No matter what feeling arises, let it be. Do not be afraid. Understand that everything that happens within you and around you is a manifestation of the Self. It is fine to have visions, but they are not necessary. The most important thing is to attain inner happiness and inner peace. That is the purpose of meditation. When all the senses become quiet and you experience bliss, you are in meditation. Meditate with this awareness: "I am not different from God, nor is God different from me." Meditate on your Self. Honor your Self. Know your Self. God dwells within you as you.

How Often to Meditate

Q: How often should I meditate?
SM: Meditation should become your daily routine. You should not live without meditating any more than you live without sleeping or eating. If you meditate every day, you will reap great fruits in the future. Do not think that the moment you sit down and close your eyes God will manifest before you. Unless you are supremely worthy, this will not happen. You have to make a disciplined daily effort. Children put coins in a piggy bank every day, and after a while they accumulate many coins. In the same way, your daily meditations will add up and bear fruit as time passes.

If You Meditate Too Much

Q: Why should we limit our meditation to an hour and a half every day?

SM: It is not that you can meditate only for an hour and a half. The point is that you have to increase the duration very gradually. You should meditate according to the capacity of your physical body. If you meditate too much, your head will become too hot. One who meditates has to eat nourishing foods. In our kitchen we use cashew nuts, clarified butter, pistachios, raisins, and other foods that give us strength.

In the marrow of the bones is a radiant yellow fluid called *ojas.* It is created from sexual fluid, and it imparts strength and the power of memory. If you meditate a great deal but do not provide your body with rich food, the fire of meditation will begin to consume that *ojas,* and then you will become tired and dull, and you will lose your enthusiasm. That is why I place a limit on meditation. If you want to meditate for long periods, you should not only eat rich food, but also be celibate and conserve your sexual fluid.

You can meditate twice a day, one hour in the morning and one hour in the evening, provided that you drink milk and eat sweet foods, such as fruit. You should be very careful about the food you eat. The meditation that comes after the Shakti has been awakened has tremendous strength; it is like a big fire. In the West people think that meditation is simple and ordinary, but the truth is that the fire of meditation burns up all impurities. Meditation purifies the nerves and vital airs, strengthens the body, and cleanses the mind. Then the mind becomes still, and one becomes established in the inner Self.

Love for Meditation

To meditate successfully, you must have genuine interest. If you have real love for meditation, you will not have to struggle to find your own innermost reality; you will discover it easily. I will tell you a story that illustrates this. Akbar was a great Moghul king of India. One day he went for a ride in the forest. When it was time for afternoon prayers, he got down from his horse, spread his mat on the side of the road, and began to pray. While he was praying, a woman passed by. Earlier that day the woman's husband had gone into the forest to gather wood. Though it was past midday, he had not yet returned, and she was feeling anxious about him. She had set out to search for him and was walking very fast, preoccupied by her concern. As she hurried along, she happened to step on Akbar's prayer mat. Akbar was furious, but he could not say anything, because in the Muslim religion one is forbidden to speak during prayers. The incident enraged him so much that he could not stop thinking about it. Instead of drinking the love of God through prayer, he was only drinking the poison of anger.

After the woman had walked a little farther, she saw her husband approaching from the opposite direction. She ran to him, threw her arms around him, and started to walk home with him. Soon they reached the place where Akbar had been praying. By then, he had finished his prayers and was shaking out his mat. When he saw the husband and wife coming toward him, the fire of his anger flared up again, and he shouted at the woman, "What sort of person are you? Don't you have any shame? Don't you have any sense of propriety?"

The woman was astonished. She did not know what she had done wrong; she was not even aware that she had stepped on Akbar's mat. "Your Majesty," she said, "will you please tell me what has happened?"

The king cried, "Don't you remember? I was trying to absorb myself in the love of the Lord, but you came along and stepped on my mat!"

"Your Majesty," the woman said, "I am terribly sorry. I was rushing to find my husband, and I was so absorbed in thoughts of him that I was not even aware that you or your prayer mat were in front of me. Still, Your Majesty, there is one thing that puzzles me. You were praying to God, who is so much greater than a mere husband. How is it that you were not more absorbed than I? How is it that you noticed me?"

You must become absorbed in your meditation as that woman was absorbed in her husband. Then it will not take you any time to reach the Self.

Meditation Teaches You Meditation

Q: What was it like when you first began to meditate?
SM: In the beginning, I meditated just as you meditate now. When I sat for meditation with my eyes closed, my mind would go here and there, thinking of one thing or another. But as I meditated more and more, I began to learn the skill of getting into meditation. I found that as I did *sadhana, sadhana* taught me *sadhana.* Meditation taught me meditation. This will happen to you, too.

The Monk and the Goddess

Q: Although I have been meditating for a year and a half, I still have had no significant experiences. Is something wrong with me, or am I expecting too much?
SM: Give up your expectations. Expectations are a great hindrance in meditation. Very often, when subtle inner experiences take place, we are not immediately aware of them. Even if nothing appears to be happening now, keep meditating and sooner or later you will experience something. Your good actions will never go to waste.

In India there lived a very intelligent and well-respected man, who was the prime minister of a king. One day he thought to himself, "Why am I doing this work? I am doing it only for money. I should give it up and simply worship Lakshmi, the goddess of wealth. Then wealth will come to me."

The next day he resigned his position and went to live by a river. Every day he repeated the mantras to Lakshmi and worshipped her according to the Vedic tradition. The Vedic rituals are very scientific. In ancient times, the sages used to worship the god of rain, and the result was that there were no droughts. In the same way, it was believed that if someone worshipped the goddess of wealth, he would be rewarded with wealth.

Twelve years went by, and not only did the prime minister not receive anything, but he used up all his money and became a beggar. Finally he thought, "This is useless. No wealth is going to come to me. I will take *sannyasa* initiation and become a monk."

So he went off and took initiation into monkhood. A few days later, he was sitting on top of a mountain, meditating. At the end of his meditation, he opened his eyes and saw a beautiful woman standing before him. She was shining as if made of gold. He was astounded by her beauty.

"What are you doing here?" he asked.

"I am here to see you," the woman said. "You invited me, and I have come."

"What are you talking about?" asked the monk. "I never invited you. I'm a monk!"

"Didn't you recite the hymns to Lakshmi for twelve years?"

"Yes."

"I am Lakshmi."

The monk prostrated before her and said, "I worshipped you for so long, but you never came. Why have you come now?"

"You had accumulated so many sins and so many *karmas* that your worship could not bear fruit. Finally, when you took *sannyasa,* all your sins were burned up and you became completely pure. That is why I have come to you now."

"But I no longer have any use for you," said the monk.

"Still, I cannot leave you," Lakshmi said. "You performed the worship, and now you have to experience its fruits."

"In that case," said the monk, "give me the wealth of knowledge."

Lakshmi agreed to do this. The monk became a storehouse of knowledge and received the name Vidyaranya, which means "the forest of knowledge." He wrote a great book called the *Panchadasi,* which is still studied by everyone who learns Sanskrit.

You never know what *karmas* are standing behind you. You have been accumulating *karmas* and impressions for many lifetimes. How can you hope to rid yourself of all of them by meditating for only a year and a half? Keep meditating regularly and stay calm. Sooner or later, through the grace of the inner Shakti, everything will happen.

That Joy Is Realization

Q: I am impatient to attain God.
SM: Which God do you want to attain, yours or someone else's?
Q: I want to attain my Self.
SM: God exists inside, so you will be able to see Him.
Q: But I have never seen any lights or had any visions in meditation.
SM: If you want to see a light, you can look at the outer sun. The same light is both outside and inside. Good meditation is seeing nothing. When seeing stops, you really experience something. It is all right to have visions, but God is that which is beyond them. The state of God is tranquil. It is a state of absolute quiet. If you want to have visions, you will have them, but having visions does not mean that your work is over. What are you experiencing when you meditate?
Q: Sometimes when I breathe in while doing the *So'ham* mantra, I feel laughter.
SM: Can you explain that state?
Q: It is a pool of laughter.
SM: That joy is realization.
Q: It lasts just one second.
SM: You should make it last longer. Joy is the true attainment. The state in which *ham* has merged within, before *so* has arisen, is the Truth. That is the mystery of the Siddhas. Its nature is joy and love. As you meditate more and more, your heart will begin to overflow with love. You will get into a state in which you laugh like one who is mad. I am not telling you to become mad; I am only telling you that love and happiness should come forth spontaneously from inside you. God is joy. He is not a mountain or a light. Traveling to different planes is mediocre. God is beyond all planes.

The Experience of a Realized Being

Q: What is the experience of a realized being? Does he experience the Self as being without attributes, or does he continue to see dazzling colors and blue light?

SM: The final experience of God is beyond all attributes; it is beyond all forms and colors. When one is in that state, the mind no longer exists to make distinctions among red, white, black, and yellow. On the road to realization one has many experiences and visions, but the experience of realization transcends all of these. It is beyond description; words cannot capture it. It has no shadow, no form, and no gender. When salt falls into the ocean, it merges in the ocean. It loses its individuality and becomes absorbed in the ocean. The final experience is like that. A saint said, "When I perceived the divine manifestation of God, I lost myself completely in Him. I do not know myself any longer." As you understand the Truth more and more, you will go beyond even the state of understanding. As you meditate on the Truth more and more, the meditator and the object of meditation will merge, and that is the state of the final experience. Sometimes people say, "I was meditating, and for a while I did not know what happened to me." That not knowing is the experience of God.

However, when a realized being is in meditation and moves just a bit out of the ultimate state, he experiences visions and very soft, beautiful lights. He sees these things when the mind is turned within but its modifications are not completely still. As soon as he goes beyond those inner modifications, he sees neither lights nor visions.

The knowers of the Truth have described two states of inner *samadhi: savikalpa,* the *samadhi* with thought; and *nirvikalpa,* the *samadhi* beyond thought. In the *savikalpa* state one experiences the Self as dazzling light and brilliant colors. In the *nirvikalpa* state even they do not exist, because there is no longer a seer.

The Highest Meditation

When you come to the end of your practice of meditation, you will realize that everything is the Self. When this is the case, why do you not realize it at the beginning and meditate with the awareness that the Self pervades everywhere? Then you will have no trouble meditating, because you will always be in meditation.

Once a disciple approached a saint and requested spiritual instruction. The saint said, "What am I to tell you? Everything is the Self. Just as water solidifies and becomes ice, the Self takes form and becomes this universe. There is nothing but that Self. You are that Self. Recognize this and you will know everything."

The seeker was not satisfied. "Is that all you have to say?" he asked. "I can read that in a book." He was puzzled because the Guru had not asked him to do hatha yoga or *pranayama,* to shave his head or grow a beard, or to meditate on a specific object. "Can't you say something else?" he asked.

"That is all I have to teach," the saint said. "If you want more instruction, you will have to go elsewhere."

So the seeker approached a second Guru and asked him for instruction. This Guru was very clever, and he knew what kind of person the seeker was. "I will instruct you," he said, "but first you will have to serve me for twelve years." In India, since ancient times, service to the Guru has been considered a great spiritual practice. It is a very mysterious *sadhana,* in which knowledge of the Truth arises spontaneously in a seeker as he works for the Guru. So the seeker willingly accepted this condition and asked the Guru what kind of service he should perform. The Guru called the manager of his ashram and asked, "What kind of job do you have for this seeker?"

"There is only one job open, and that is picking up buffalo dung," answered the manager.

"Will you do that?" the Guru asked.

"Yes," said the seeker.

The seeker was very sincere and true, so he did not question the nature of the work. He was willing to spend twelve years picking up buffalo dung, because he considered the experience of the Self to be worth any kind of effort. Day in and day out for twelve years he picked up buffalo dung. Then one day he looked at the calendar and discovered that he had worked for twelve years and two days, so he went to the Guru and said, "I have finished my twelve years of service. Please give me instruction."

The Guru said, "This is my teaching: Everything is Consciousness. The Self alone appears as all things in the universe. You, too, are the very same Self."

Because of his years of *sadhana,* the seeker had become very ripe, and as soon as he heard the Guru's words he went into a deep *samadhi,* during which he experienced the Truth. But when he came out he said, "O Guruji, one thing puzzles me. I already received this teaching. It is the same teaching the other Guru gave me."

"Yes," said the Guru. "The Truth doesn't change in twelve years."

"Then why did I have to pick up buffalo dung for such a long time in order to understand it?"

"Because you were stupid," the Guru replied.

This is the truth. If you had a keen intellect and the power of understanding and discrimination, what spiritual practices would you need to perform in order to recognize your own Self? How much time would it take you to experience that Consciousness which is manifest everywhere? It is just a matter of recognition, and it is so simple that it takes only a fraction of a second.

It is only because you do not have this power of understanding that you have to meditate. For so many years, you have been living in the awareness "I am an individual," and for this reason it is very difficult for you to immediately accept the awareness "I am God." You have been filling your mind with negative thoughts and feelings about other people and about yourself, thinking that you are small, that you are weak, that you are sinful. You have spent your life trapped in limited identification. If your body is beautiful, you think that you are beautiful, whereas if your body is ugly, you think that you are ugly. If you study, you consider yourself learned, whereas if you do not study, you consider yourself illiterate. When anger, greed, and attachment arise in you, you identify yourself with them. This is ego, the sense of limited individuality, which has trapped you for innumerable lifetimes.

To rid yourself of this limited "I"-sense, to purify your mind and heart so that you can accept the awareness "I am Consciousness," you have to meditate, repeat the mantra, and perform good actions. But if you really want these things to bear fruit, you should do them with the awareness of your identity with Consciousness. You should practice the *sadhana* of Shiva, the *sadhana* of identification with the Truth.[9] You should keep your mind immersed in the idea of *Shivo'ham*, "I am Shiva," and *So'ham*, "I am That." You should have this understanding: "It is God who is meditating. All the objects of my meditation are God. My meditation itself is God." When you have this awareness, then you can practice your *sadhana* anywhere and at any time. You will not have to close your eyes or still your mind, because when you have this awareness, even the ordinary activities of your daily life will become meditation, and you will begin to experience the Truth spontaneously, whatever you are doing.

Meditation in the World

Many people feel that if they want to pursue meditation and spiritual life, they will have to leave their jobs and families and go off to a cave somewhere and sit like a log. But when a person understands that the Self pervades everywhere, he realizes that there is no difference between mundane life and spiritual life. Then he does not have to give up his family. He does not have to leave his job. He does not have to retreat from society. Kashmir Shaivism says, *Nashivam vidyate kvachit*—"Nothing exists which is not Shiva." For this reason, no activity in this world is an obstacle on the spiritual path as long as a person does it with love and with the awareness that the Self dwells in all.[10] A musician can pursue the Self while creating music, provided that he does it without selfish motivation. A teacher can pursue the Self through teaching, provided that he teaches selflessly. A businessman can pursue the Self while doing business, provided that he does it without selfish desire. A mother can pursue the Self while raising her children, provided that she does it selflessly. No matter what your field of activity, if you dedicate your work to God, it becomes a spiritual practice. If you simply do your work without personal desire for its fruits, that too is a great yoga.

The truth is that when a person meditates on the Self, he feels more love for the world; he has more interest in it and more understanding of it. As long as you lack knowledge, this world will merely be a world for you, and every action merely an action. But when you attain true knowledge, you will realize that whatever you do is meditation and worship of the Self. In one of his hymns, Shankaracharya sang, *Sanchārah padayoh pradakshinavidhih stotrāni sarvā giro; yadyatkarma karomi tattadakhilam shambho tavārādhanam*[11]—"O Lord, wherever I go, I am walking around You. Whatever I do is worship of You." This is true understanding, and this is the awareness with which you should practice *sadhana.* If you can recognize that everything you see, inside and outside, is nothing but your own Self, then at every moment you will be in meditation.

Notes

1. *Bhagavad Gita,* XIII.24.
2. See *Chandogya Upanishad,* VII.6.1.
3. See *Shiva Sutras,* I.1: *Chaitanyam ātmā.*
4. *Kena Upanishad,* I.6.
5. See Patanjali, *Yoga Sutras,* I.2: *Yogash chitta vritti nirodaha*—"Yoga is to still the ripples of the mind"; I.3: *Tadā drashtuhu svarūpe'vasthānam*—"Then the seer is established in his own essential nature."
6. Ibid., I.27–29.
7. Ibid., II.46: *Sthira-sukham āsanam*—"A posture [should be] steady and comfortable."
8. Jnaneshwar Maharaj describes these as follows: "The whole body is like a lotus which has four petals of four kinds, colors, and sizes. Each of these has its own significance. The first is the gross body; its color is red. The second petal is the subtle body, in which we sleep and experience dreams. It is the size of a thumb, and its color is white. The third petal is the causal body. It is the size of the tip of the third finger, and its color is black. The fourth petal is the supracausal body, which is as small as a sesame seed. Its color is blue. This last body is of the greatest importance. It is very brilliant; it is the foundation of *sadhana;* it is the highest inner vision."
9. See Somananda, *Shiva Drishti,* VII.96–98: *Shivo'smi sādhanā visthtaha shivo'ham yājako'pyaham, /shivam yāmi shivo yami shivena shiva*

sādhanaha—"Practice *sadhana* with the following awareness: 'I am a form of Shiva. I will attain Shiva. By becoming Him, I will attain Him. Because I am Shiva, I will attain Shivahood very easily.' "

10. Ibid., VII.100: *Shivaha kartā shivaha karma shivo'smi karanātmakaha*—"Shiva is the doer of everything, and He is also the action. Although I am involved with all my senses, I am still Shiva."
11. *Shiva Manasa Puja.*

THE GURU

He is the real Guru
Who can reveal the form of the formless
  before your eyes;
Who teaches the simple path,
  without rites or ceremonies;
Who does not make you close your doors,
  and hold your breath,
  and renounce the world;
Who makes you perceive
  the Supreme Spirit
  wherever the mind attaches itself;
Who teaches you to be still
  in the midst of all your activities.
Fearless, always immersed in bliss,
  he keeps the spirit of yoga
  in the midst of enjoyments.

— Kabir

What Is a True Guru?

When I was pursuing my *sadhana,* I followed many teachers and many paths. I read a great deal about saints and came to the conclusion that I could know my own inner Self only with the help of a Guru. And that was true: I received everything from my Guru, and even now I receive blessings from him. That is why I always say that there is nothing greater or more valuable than the Guru.

Today the Guru market is booming, because more and more people have a thirst for spirituality. But despite the growing interest in Gurus, opposition to Gurus is also on the rise. Because of the behavior of false Gurus—those who call themselves Gurus without having had a Guru of their own—some people become very upset whenever they hear the word "Guru."

Sheikh Nasrudin lived in a time that was ripe for Gurus. There was no Guru in his town, so the townspeople went to him and said, "Nasrudin, we would like you to become our Guru." Nasrudin accepted their offer. "My first instruction is this," he said. "Tomorrow we will all get together and go fishing."

If a person assumes the role of Guru without being a true Guru, what can he do but take you fishing?

There are imitations among people in every field, so it should not be surprising that there are also imitations among Gurus. This does not mean that every Guru is false. Nonetheless, it is very good to be mistrustful of Gurus, because in this way we exercise our discrimination and learn how to choose a real Guru. A great being said that by being in the company of thieves one can learn how to tell the difference between a thief and an honest man. In the same way, by observing a false Guru we can learn the qualities of a real one.

Why do false Gurus exist? It is our own fault. We choose our Gurus just as we choose our politicians. The false Guru market is growing because the false disciple market is growing. Because of his blind selfishness, a false Guru drowns people, and because of *his* blind selfishness and wrong understanding, a false disciple gets trapped. A true disciple would never be trapped by a false Guru.

False disciples want a Guru from whom they can attain something cheaply and easily. They want a Guru who can give them instant *samadhi.* They do not want a Guru who follows discipline and self-control; they want one who will participate in their own licentious lives. They want a Guru who is just like they are—who will practice therapy with them, who will dance with them, who will drink with them, and who will encourage them to take drugs. But one who behaves in this way can never be a true Guru. Gold is gold. It will never turn itself into brass.

A Guru is not someone who pops up from somewhere and dispenses teachings. A Guru is not someone who goes into a forest and contemplates, has a vision, and then comes back into the world to give people knowledge. A Guru is not someone who has adopted a variety of techniques from here and there and claims that one can attain the Truth by pursuing all of them. A Guru is not someone who says, "I have a lot of knowledge and you are all ignorant, so come and receive my teachings."

In fact, the Guru is not a human being at all. The word "Guru" actually refers to the creator of the glory of this world.[1] In Kashmir Shaivism it is said that God performs five actions: creation, sustenance, dissolution, concealment, and bestowal of grace. The *Shiva Sutra Vimarshini* says, *Gururvā pārameshwarī anugrahikā shaktihi*[2]— "The Guru is God's grace-bestowing power." In other words, the Guru is not an individual, but the divine power of grace flowing through that individual. That power is the same Shakti which creates and supports the world.

The Guru principle has not come into existence recently. It existed even before the universe was created, and just like water, earth, air, fire, and ether, it has been a part of creation ever since it began.[3] The Guru principle is within everyone as the inner Self, so when we pay our respects to the Guru, we are paying our respects to our own Self. The Guru is the Self; he is nothing but supreme Consciousness and supreme bliss.

The Qualifications of a Guru

A true Guru comes from the lineage of Gurus founded by Parashiva, the supreme Guru. That is why when you meet a Guru, the first question you should ask is, "Who was his Guru?" Before you put your trust in an engineer or a professor, you inquire, "From which university did he get his diploma?" In the same way, before you accept a Guru, you should know what his lineage is. In his book *The Serpent Power,* the great scholar Sir John Woodroffe wrote that trying to be a Guru without first having had a Guru is like trying to ride a train without a ticket. A person can become a Guru only after receiving a command from his own Guru. The lineage of Gurus should be alive in him.

A Guru must meet other qualifications. He should be learned; he should have studied many scriptures and spiritual philosophies, and he should know them perfectly. The knowledge of the ancient scriptural authors was unsurpassed. They practiced their *sadhana* completely and wrote books only after having fully realized the Truth. Today people write books according to their own ideas, but what is the foundation of these books? What philosophical system supports them? A person who writes such books cannot be a true Guru; he can only spread his own delusion. Shiva told Brahmadeva, "He who indulges in mere reasoning, who entangles his disciples in a net of gossip, complicated words, and arguments can never be a true Guru." A genuine Guru has full knowledge of the Truth embodied in the Upanishads and other great scriptures, and his teaching is the same as the teaching of the ancient sages.

But it is not enough for a Guru to know the scriptures. He must also be well versed in mundane arts and skills. He must be knowledgeable about every area of life. It is all right if an ear specialist knows only about the ear or if a heart specialist is an expert only on the heart. But a Guru cannot be a specialist in just one area. If a Guru is to guide seekers who are living in the world, he must be familiar with all their joys and all their problems.

A Guru must also have had the direct experience of God. A true Guru has seen God just as one sees any object in the outer world. By meditating on the supreme Truth, he has experienced that Truth within himself and has merged his individuality into it. As a result, he no longer sees the world as a material phenomenon, but as the light of pure Consciousness. He sees that light sparkling and scintillating in men and women, in children, in animals and trees, and in himself. To him, both matter and consciousness are only different grades of Consciousness, for he sees nothing but Consciousness everywhere.

Not only is a true Guru enlightened; he can also give the experience of enlightenment to others. Because he has become one with Consciousness, the power of Consciousness has taken up residence in him, simply for the bestowal of grace. It is said that just as many lights are kindled by a single flame, the Guru's Shakti can kindle the inner Shakti of many disciples.[4] The force of the divine Self, pulsating within every human being, is constantly flowing out of the body. But the Guru has stored this energy inside himself and can transmit it to others. Rays of Consciousness emanate from every part of him, and anyone who comes in contact with him can receive his Shakti.

The Guru also has the power to control the intensity of the awakened Shakti. If the energy is working too strongly in a disciple, the Guru can reduce the level of its intensity. If it is not working strongly enough, he can increase it. He can sustain the process he initiated in the disciple, remove all the disciple's inner blocks, and make joy arise within him.[5] He can guarantee that the awakened Shakti will ultimately lead the disciple to the highest state. The Guru has realized the potency of the mantra, and he can also make the disciple realize its potency.[6] The power of the Siddha lineage fully supports the Guru, and once a seeker has received Shakti, the lineage also stands behind him, protecting him as he moves toward the goal.

The Guru is absolutely necessary in one's life—as necessary as the vital force. The great saint Sunderdas said, "Without the Guru there is no meditation. No high knowledge can arise without him. There is no love without the Guru, no wealth without the Guru, no equanimity of mind without the Guru, and no illumination of the intellect without the Guru." The syllable *gu* means "darkness" and the syllable *ru* means "light";[7] a true Guru dispels the disciple's ignorance and bestows light. He takes away the disciple's wrong understanding, his delusion of imperfection, and grants him the highest wisdom.

The Guru is not interested in collecting money from his disciples, but only in increasing their good qualities and eliminating their shortcomings.[8] He does not need anything from anyone, because he has everything he wants within himself. His eyes are not attracted by beautiful forms, nor is his tongue infatuated with delicious flavors, nor do his ears long to hear sweet sounds. He is completely free from the pull of the senses; because he is constantly drinking the ecstasy of the inner Self, his senses have turned within and take delight only in that inner ecstasy.[9] Unlike the mind of an ordinary person, the mind of the Guru is always steady. Just as a flame does not flicker where there is no wind, the Guru's mind never moves from the Self. The Guru is as deep and serene as the ocean. In his heart there is only compassion and love for all beings; there is no desire, anger, pride, or jealousy. For him, all religions, all actions, all countries, and all beings are equal.

He is established in his own teachings, and even though he has completed his *sadhana,* he himself always practices the teachings he imparts to others. He never breaks his own discipline. He follows strict celibacy, and as a result his sexual fluid always flows upward; it is through the power of the upward-flowing sexual fluid that he is able to give *shaktipat*. Although he lives in a state beyond such concepts as virtue and sin, the Guru observes righteous conduct, and simply by being in his company a disciple begins to observe good conduct. What can a disciple gain by following someone who is not disciplined and pure? A disciple can benefit only from one who teaches the perfect path, whose company uplifts him, and through whom he experiences revolutionary changes within himself. If he lives with such a being, or spends time in his presence, or even listens to his lectures, he will be transformed automatically, without any struggle. Tukaram Maharaj said, "The glory of the Guru is unfathomable. Even to compare him to the philosophers' stone is not enough. The philosophers' stone has the power to turn base metal into gold, yet it cannot turn it into a philosophers' stone. A true Guru, however, can turn a disciple into a Guru like himself."

The Guru is our supreme benefactor. He destroys our confusion and shows us our true nature and the purpose of our lives. He helps us to develop love for God and reveals God to us from within. The mystery of the Guru is very great. Just by keeping his company, we can experience God directly. Ekanath Maharaj said, "O my friend, since I received the lotion of the Guru's grace, I see only God wherever I look. Inside I see God, outside I see God. Whatever I see in this world is only God." This is the power of the Guru's grace.

The Eye to See the Self

Q: If I decide that I want to know my own Self, why do I need a teacher, since I am essentially in dialogue with myself?
SM: Can you tell me what you have ever learned in your life without someone's help? You learned how to walk from your parents. You learned from them how to utter even simple words such as "Mommy" and "Daddy." In elementary and high school you learned everything from your teachers, and in college you learned everything from your professors. In the same way, you have to learn about the Self from a Guru. If you were able to know the Self on your own, I would thank

you, because then I could tell others that they, too, could know the Self without help.

I don't force you to have a Guru, nor do I insist that you be with a Guru all the time. I tell you to know your own Self. If you could know your Self without a Guru, believe me, it would be a great help to me. But the truth is that to understand the Self you must have someone who can show it to you. It is very easy to know others but very difficult to know your own Self. The world is full of scientists, psychologists, artists, dancers, and others with various skills and talents. Even though they may be adept at their professions, how many of these people know themselves?

To know your Self, you have to reach the true center of your being. When you look at yourself in a mirror, you will see your hair only if you look at your hair. You will see your eyes only if you look at your eyes. You will not see any part of your body in a mirror if you do not look at it. In the same way, to see your own Self you have to know where to look. For this you need a teacher, a guide.

A Guru is not useless or meaningless. If people think that a Guru is unnecessary, it is either because certain Gurus make themselves useless in people's eyes, or because people don't understand the Guru, and so misuse him and then consider him useless.

Q: Many people think that by following a Guru they will be allowing their lives to fall under someone else's control.

SM: A Guru doesn't make a person weak and keep him under his control. Instead, he frees him from dependency. The job of a Guru is not to bind a disciple, but to give him the freedom of the Self. People think that if they accept the authority of a Guru, they will lose their individual freedom and become slaves. But when they fall sick, they don't think that they are compromising their individual freedom by going to a doctor. When their financial situation is bad, they don't think that they are compromising their freedom by getting a bank loan. If their craving for taste becomes strong, they don't mind eating all kinds of delicious foods, and if their eyes want satisfaction, they don't mind watching all kinds of movies. They don't consider these things to be dependence, but when it comes to turning to a Guru or God, they immediately raise the question of loss of freedom. I don't understand this kind of thinking. When I took refuge in my Guru, I became completely free of dependence.

Q: But if I learn language from a language teacher or mathematics from a mathematics teacher, I learn it according to the teacher's belief system. I don't learn anything about me; I learn only the teacher's view of the world. Doesn't that happen with the Guru? Don't I come to know the Guru's view of the world rather than discovering my own?

SM: The Guru's outlook is not something imposed on you from outside. If you go to an optician, he doesn't give you the prescription of his glasses. He gives you a prescription that is right for you. In the same way, the Guru's outlook is the viewpoint of the Self. He gives you the eye to see the Self.

Q: Throughout history there have been many leaders who brought their followers to destruction. I am sure those followers felt that they had chosen the right teacher for them.

SM: If they were destroyed, there was some defect in their way of choosing. This is why a person who is choosing a Guru should be very alert and intelligent. He has to ask himself a few questions: "Who made this Guru a Guru? Is he doing business as a Guru, or does he really follow spiritual discipline? What is the purpose of his teachings? By being with him have I learned my own value and the value of others? Have I acquired the knowledge of universal brotherhood? Do his teachings plunge me into deeper confusion and increase my bondage, or do they take me higher?" A seeker should reflect on all of these things.

One needs the right eye in order to recognize a true Guru. There is a beautiful Indian saying about Gurus: "Before you drink water, strain it very well; before you accept a Guru, check him carefully." Accept a Guru only after you know him very well. Do not accept someone as a Guru just because you have been told that he is a Guru. Never have blind faith.

The Water of a Cobbler

In the state of Rajasthan, in India, lived a cobbler named Ravidas, who was a great Siddha. Many people used to go to him, and in his company they would experience peace and happiness. The prime minister of the state heard of Ravidas and went to see him. Filled with peace, he returned to the palace and told the king, "There is a great saint living in the city. I am sure that if you go to him he will be able to give you some peace."

This king was very unhappy. He had a great deal of wealth and power and all the other things that make a person agitated. He did not have anything that gave him peace. But when the prime minister suggested that he go to Ravidas, he began to grumble. "He is a cobbler," he said. "How can a king ask for instructions from a cobbler?" But the prime minister persisted, "Your Majesty, you are so restless. I am sure that Ravidas can help you." At last, the king agreed to go to the saint. He waited until there was a big holiday in the city. When he was sure that everyone was at the celebration, he disguised himself and went to Ravidas's shop. He walked inside, saluted the saint, and said, "I am very unhappy and I lack peace. Please give me something that will bring peace to my heart."

Ravidas was an omniscient being. He knew who the king was, and he knew the state of the king's mind. Next to his workbench, he kept a stone pot full of water into which he dipped pieces of leather before he worked them. Ravidas poured some of this water into a glass and gave it to the king. "Drink this," he said.

When the king saw the water, which was dark red and smelled like leather, he was disgusted. "I am a king," he thought. "Why have I come here anyway?" He turned his back to the saint and pretended to be drinking, but instead he poured the water down his shirt. Then he quickly bowed to the saint and left.

When the king returned to the palace, he saw that his shirt was badly stained, so he called the royal washerman and told him to wash it. The washerman was surprised to see the king's shirt in such condition. After making several inquiries, he found out that the king had gone to see Ravidas and that he had poured the water from Ravidas's stone pot onto his shirt. He gave the shirt to his daughter, explained to her what had happened, and told her to wash the shirt very well.

The daughter was very intelligent and very pure, and she knew Ravidas's power. So she took the shirt and sucked out all the stains. Then she washed it and gave it back to her father to return to the king.

From that day on, the girl had very deep meditations, and her state became higher and higher. After a few years, she had attained such a high state that people began to feel the same joy in her presence that they felt in the company of Ravidas. Many people went to receive her blessings, and among them was the prime minister. After he had seen her, he went to the king and said, "O Your Majesty, you are still so unhappy and agitated. Why don't you go to that ecstatic girl and see if she can give you some peace?" The king was reluctant—after all, she was merely the daughter of a washerman—yet his restlessness was causing him great pain. Finally, he overcame his reluctance and went to the girl's room. He stood before her and said, "I am very unhappy and I lack peace. Please give me your blessing so that I can attain peace."

The girl looked at him with great wonderment. "O Your Majesty," she said. "Everything I have, I received from what you threw away. Everything I have, I obtained by sucking Ravidas's water out of the shirt you gave my father to wash!"

This is the value of the Guru's grace. To attain the Truth from him, we do not have to receive instructions. It is enough simply to imbibe his Shakti. But first we must understand its value.

The Destiny of Saints

Q: Are all fully realized beings Gurus?

SM: All fully realized beings are not Gurus. Some become Gurus, and some remain withdrawn from the world. Even though the inner state of all realized beings is the same, their outer actions differ according to their destiny and the austerities they have performed. For example, Janaka was a great king who had 700 queens, but his disciple Shuka was a renunciant who was always naked. Although Hanuman attained the same knowledge as Janaka and Shuka, he remained a servant. Vasishtha expounded meditation, but he himself was always engaged in performing rituals.

Bartruhari said that it is very difficult to understand the ways of great beings. Some act like saints, others like madmen, and others like ghosts. Some remain naked, using the earth as a bed. Others live like kings, surrounded by wealth and luxury. Some are completely serene and never speak. Others go around swearing. Some are very active. Others lie like pythons and never move. But no matter how they behave, all of these Siddhas have attained the same state of inner perfection. Just by coming in contact with them, seekers are uplifted.

In the state of Maharashtra, near my ashram, lived a great being called Nana Aulia. He used to lie on the road all day, but no one would ever bother him because everyone knew that he was a saint. One day the district officer of the region came driving by in a horse-drawn carriage. When the driver saw Nana Aulia lying in the middle of the road, he stopped the carriage. The district officer was outraged. He said to the driver, "Tell that idiot to get off the road!"

"I am not going to tell him anything," replied the driver. "You can tell him if you want to." So the officer got down from the carriage, went over to the great being, and shook him. "Get up!" he shouted. "You're blocking the road!" With that, Nana Aulia stood up and slapped the district officer in the face. In an instant, the officer's understanding changed. He got back into the carriage, returned to town, and resigned his position. Later, he became a great saint.

So there are some realized beings who do not specifically function as Gurus but have attained the state of Guruhood. Even if they do not give instructions, their actions have the power to turn one in a spiritual direction.

The Guru's Presence

Q: Many of your disciples attest to experiencing you when you are not physically present. This seems to be an ordinary and natural occurrence in the relationship between Guru and disciple. Are you consciously aware of it?

SM: It is very true that even when I am not physically present, my disciples experience my presence. That is because I have become one with the Shakti. The Shakti pervades the entire world, from the east to the west, from the north to the south, above and below, and it hasn't excluded anyone. Because I exist within my disciples in the form of the awakened Shakti, they can experience my presence everywhere and at all times, no matter where they live. I do not have to guide them, because they receive guidance from the inner Shakti. If I had to guide my disciples personally, then this would not be divine work. It would not be spontaneous yoga.

Being with the Guru

Q: How much is our spiritual growth accelerated if we are constantly with the Guru physically?

SM: If you are with the Guru physically, your *sadhana* will progress quickly. However, you have to think about what it means to be with the Guru. It is useless to stay with him and just go on doing whatever you like. If you hold on to your anger and increase your negative feelings, what is the use of being with him? You can attain the highest state only if you follow the teachings of your Guru, constantly repeat the mantra he has given to you, and feel your oneness with him. Only then can you say that you are with the Guru physically.

What you really need to increase the power of your *sadhana* is not proximity to the Guru's physical form, but love. If you have love for the Guru and for the Self, then you can imbibe Shakti from the Guru, and that Shakti will take you to the highest state. The greatest *sadhana* is love, nothing but love.

Opening Oneself

Q: It is difficult to open oneself to another person, but it is even more difficult to open oneself to a Guru. How can we learn to open up and love him?
SM: First of all, it is not the physical form of the Guru that you should love, but his teachings and his path. You do not have to do anything to open yourself to the Guru. Just follow the path that he shows. Eventually you will experience something on that path, and then very naturally you will come to love the Guru. To love a Guru does not mean to follow after him, saying, "O Guru, Guru, Guru." A true Guru would never encourage this. All you have to do is follow his teachings.

The True Relationship

Q: All over the world, a large number of people are following different Gurus. Would you say that they all experience the true Guru – disciple relationship? What determines that relationship?
SM: If a disciple meets a Guru and is completely transformed, the relationship is true.
Q: Is that transformation apparent to others?
SM: If someone has experienced that inner transformation, others can see it because his attitude and behavior have changed. His mind is free of agitation, his heart is filled with joy, and he is very friendly. However, some people never change. They go to an ashram, stay for a while, and are the same when they leave.

The Disciple

Truly speaking, the Guru never takes and he never gives. He is always tranquil. The disciple has to elicit the Shakti of the Guru through his faith and love. He has to approach the Guru with the attitude of discipleship. Everywhere I go people ask me this question: "Baba, when does a person receive the grace of the Guru?" And I always say, "Only when the disciple bestows his grace on the Guru can the Guru bestow his on the disciple." If the disciple does not bestow his favor, how can the Guru give his blessing? If the disciple's grace is there, it will attract the Guru's grace. But if there is no discipleship, the teachings of the Guru cannot take root.

Once a seeker went to the great Sufi Guru Dho'l-Nun and asked him for teachings. "Can you stay with me for a few days?" the Guru asked.

"I don't have time," said the seeker. "I want the teachings right away."

"Very well," said Dho'l-Nun. "There is a great being who lives across the river. Go to him and he will give you the teachings." He handed the seeker a small box and said, "Carry this box to the saint and tell him that you have come from me. But make sure that you take good care of the box and its contents."

The seeker took the box and set out for the river. When he was halfway there, he began to hear something squeaking inside the box. By the time he reached the river, he was overcome by curiosity, so he opened the box and looked inside. A small mouse jumped out and ran away. The seeker saw that it would be useless to try to recapture the mouse, so he closed the box and continued on his way. When he reached the house of the great being, he handed him the box and said, "I have been sent to you by Dho'l-Nun. He told me that you would be able to give me teachings."

The great being opened the box and looked inside. "Wasn't there something in this box?" he asked.

"Yes," said the seeker, "there was a mouse in the box, but on the way here I opened the box, and the mouse jumped out."

"What did Dho'l-Nun tell you?" the saint asked. "Didn't he tell you to take care of the box and its contents? If you can't even take care of a small mouse, how will you be able to take care of these great teachings? Get out!"

Going to a Guru is not like going to a pizza parlor, where one can order a pizza and expect to get it within ten minutes. To obtain the Guru's Shakti and make it unfold, a disciple has to do *sadhana* with faith. If he has complete faith when the Guru transmits the Shakti into him, and if he faithfully follows the path laid down by the Guru, his inner fire will be kindled and will blaze. But if a disciple does not imbibe the Guru's teachings with firm faith, if he does not make an effort to follow the path the Guru has shown, he will not receive the Guru's blessings in full measure. That is why it is said that the Guru is the one who shows the right path, and the disciple is the one who walks on that path. If the two come together, God reveals Himself.

How to Live with the Guru

Q: Would you share with us some of your *sadhana* experiences with your Guru, Nityananda?

SM: Nityananda helped me a great deal in my *sadhana.* He was especially helpful in crushing my ego. I was considered a scholar because I had read some books and had some knowledge of the scriptures. So I had the pride of that knowledge. Above all, I wore the clothes of a *sannyasi,* and I was always playing that role. Nityananda must have undergone a lot of trouble trying to straighten me out. But he did it.

He had his own ways of testing me. Sometimes he would allow me to come close to him, and sometimes he would not. Devotees would bring him piles of sweets and fruits, which he would then distribute as *prasad.* I would get into the line of people waiting for *prasad,* but sometimes when he saw me he would hold the fruit aside and say, "No, not for you." He would do that in front of all those people, but I would not run away feeling that he had insulted me. I would just remain tranquil, thinking, "If I get something, that's fine; and if I don't get anything, that's fine too." With that attitude I spent many years with my Guru. Then one day he called me to him and said, "Go to Suki." So I went to the village of Suki and did my *sadhana* there under a tree, and through his grace I attained everything.

Sometimes when I came to see him, he would suddenly start joking about me in front of several other people. Even when the Guru teases a disciple, he is really praising him. He teases the disciple just to work on him. Sometimes my Guru would tell people all about my faults. He did this so that I would learn how to bear blame.

The more my Guru tested me, the more I advanced in my *sadhana.* No matter how much he tested me, I did not start looking for faults in him. Instead, I looked for my own faults. I asked myself, "What do I lack? What are my shortcomings?"

To live for a long time with the Guru, a disciple must have great endurance. Nowadays, people meet a Guru in the morning and by evening think that they have become Gurus themselves. But this is not how the Guru–disciple relationship works. Before a Guru makes his disciple a Guru, he tests him again and again. As long as the disciple has not discarded all his bad qualities and acquired good ones, as long as he has not achieved self-control, the Guru will keep working on him. Only the Guru knows how to work on his disciple. For this reason, it is difficult to live with the Guru. But if the disciple can make it, he will become a Guru himself.

Perfection Fills You Completely

Q: After the nine years of your *sadhana* with Swami Nityananda, how did you know that you had reached the level of completion?

SM: Everyone knows what condition he is in. When someone is incomplete, he is aware of his incompleteness. In the same way, through the same intellect, he discovers that he has become perfect.

Q: Did perfection come in an instant, or was there a gradual realization of it?

SM: One experiences that state of perfection immediately and suddenly. Then one practices *sadhana* for a while, until one becomes completely established in that state.

Q: Then you didn't need Swami Nityananda to tell you that you had had this experience? It was something you recognized inside your own being?

SM: One does recognize it within.

Q: What kind of being was Swami Nityananda? I know that he had a Guru, but was he born in a state of yoga?
SM: Yes, he was born a Siddha.
Q: What was it like to be with him? What were some of his qualities?
SM: He was in a very strange state, as you can tell by looking at his photographs. He was an *avadhut,* a being who is completely beyond conventions. He was totally free of care, and he was always intoxicated. His eyes were filled with intoxication—his entire body was filled with intoxication. He would speak very little, and even when he did speak, his words were so strange that it was hard to understand them.

He had gone beyond the mind, yet he had not become inert. He was very conscious of everything. He knew each of the thousands of people who came to visit him. He knew everything that was happening in the world. He knew the past, the present, and the future. Yet he behaved as if he knew nothing. He had equal vision. He did not consider anyone impure, low, or ignorant, nor did he consider anyone pure, great, or intelligent. He did not see good or bad in anything. If someone approached him very humbly, he would talk to him openly and give him instructions. But if anyone who was proud of his scholarship or his riches and power came to him, he would close his eyes, turn away, and become very quiet.

There was nothing in the world that could attract him. People used to bring him many things, but he never took any interest in them. The atmosphere around him was always very quiet. Thousands of people would sit with him, and just by watching him they would feel his presence inside themselves and experience knowledge arising within. Without talking, he gave instructions. Without giving the touch, he awakened the inner Shakti. Without answering people's questions verbally, he gave them the answers they needed. Without giving lectures, he gave knowledge of the Truth.

A being like my Guru does not have to give lectures. In any case, one cannot attain the Truth from lectures. Scriptures, books, and lectures are like road maps which point the way to the Truth. But to experience that Truth, to attain perfection, one needs the grace of the Guru. Through his power the Guru makes his disciple perfect.

Q: Since Swami Nityananda had this perfection from birth, it doesn't seem that he had to rely on another Siddha for attainment. Does this mean that he began a new line of the Siddha tradition or created a great wave of new grace?

SM: It was not a new wave. Nityananda continued in the tradition of the Siddha lineage. Lord Krishna and Lord Rama were both divine incarnations, but they had to receive teachings from a Guru. Though he was born a Siddha, Swami Nityananda also studied with a Guru.

Q: What was it like when you received *shaktipat* from Nityananda after twenty-four years of wandering throughout India?

SM: When I received *shaktipat,* my understanding of myself completely changed, and I had the experience "I am the supreme Truth." When a prince is sleeping, he may dream that he is a beggar, but when he wakes up he remembers that he is really a prince. That was what my initial experience was like. Then I practiced *sadhana* for a long time, until finally I became established in that experience.

Q: When you first saw Nityananda, could you see anything unusual about him, or was he able to veil his power so that you knew his greatness only when he transmitted the Shakti?

SM: I knew him for a long time, and I knew that he was a great being. Although I met him when I was fifteen years old, he did not give me *shaktipat* until much later. A Guru waits until the disciple can handle the Shakti. Then when the time is right, he gives what he has to give, and the disciple becomes perfect. So Nityananda waited until I was completely ready. Usually when one keeps the company of a great Guru, one automatically becomes ready in the course of time.

Q: So during the twenty-four years you spent wandering through India, you felt that he was with you in some deep sense?

SM: Yes, I did. From the time that I met him I had great love for him. Even when I was wandering, I would occasionally go and see him.

Q: What was it like when, as a boy of fifteen, you saw him for the first time?
SM: The moment I saw him I knew that he was a great sage. I had total faith in him.
Q: Where was that first meeting?
SM: He came to my school. He loved children. Whenever he walked by the school, all the children would run after him and walk with him for a while.
Q: What was his appearance at that time?
SM: He wore only a loincloth. In those days, many people followed him, so he would never stay in one place for very long. He would never even sit down; he would only wander and wander. Sometimes he would climb up onto the branch of a tree, and when crowds gathered beneath him, he would throw down leaves. People would gather the leaves and use them as medicine.
Q: After you reached the state of perfection, you stayed for about five more years with Nityananda before he left his body. During those years, what further development did you go through, if any?
SM: Once the state of perfection is attained it does not change. The feeling of being one with the Guru always remains. Although I had finished my *sadhana,* I knew that Nityananda was my Guru, and I identified myself only as his disciple. I lived a very simple life. I behaved like an ordinary seeker. I did not conduct any programs. Only after my Guru left his body did I start this work. The day before he left his body, he called me to him. He stroked my head for a long time. Then he put his hand into my mouth and transmitted something into me.
Q: If you were already perfect, what was it that he gave you?
SM: When a rich man is about to die, he prepares a will stating that his earnings should go to his son. In the same way, a Guru has a bundle that has been passed through the lineage, and usually when he is about to leave his body, he gives it to his disciple.
Q: So in a way, you are a treasure house containing all of Nityananda's power as well as your own.
SM: Both Shaktis are the same.

Q: Does the Guru give this final gift to his main successor or to several disciples?
SM: He gives perfection to many, but he gives the final bundle to only one.
Q: Would you describe what it felt like to have the final treasure placed inside you?
SM: There are no words for that experience. To understand it you would have to live with me and learn the language that could describe it. In that language there is only stillness. You experience perfection when you are already perfect, and you lose yourself in that perfection. It fills you completely. You experience your all-pervasiveness, and your individuality is destroyed.
Q: Did Baba Nityananda ever give you any indication that you would be the instrument to spread the tradition of *shaktipat* to so many countries?
SM: Yes, he told me that the day before he left his body.
Q: What, precisely, did he say to you?
SM: He said, "The entire world will see you one day." Some of the other things he told me are very secret. Such things are revealed only to the disciple on the final day.
Q: Again, this makes me feel that there was something unique about Baba Nityananda. After all, the Siddha tradition has existed for centuries in India, but he was perhaps the first to choose an instrument to take it around the world.
SM: Such a time sometimes comes.

Notes

1. Many verses in the Indian scriptures make this point. See *Guru Gita*, v. 89: *Brahmānandam paramasukhadam/kevalam jnāna mūrtim/dvandvātītam gaganasadrusham/tattvamasyādilakshyam;/ekam nityam vimala machalam/sarvadhisākshibhūtam/bhāvātītam trigunarahitam/sadgurum tam namāmi*—"I bow to the Sadguru, the embodiment of the bliss of the Absolute, the bestower of the highest joy. He is knowledge personified. He is beyond duality, formless, the object of Vedantic proclamations such as 'Thou art That.' He is the one Absolute. He is eternal, pure, immovable, the witness of all intellects. He transcends all mental conditions as well as the three qualities of nature."

   The *Yogashika Upanishad* says, *Yathā guru stathaivesho yathaiveshastathā guruhu*—"The Guru is God, and God is the Guru."

   The *Kularnava Tantra* says, *Tasmāt shri guru rupena*—"I [Shiva] enter the Guru and assume his form"; *gururupam samādāya bhava pāshanni kruntaye*—"Assuming the form of the Guru, I [Shiva] cut the noose of worldliness" (XIII.66).

2. Kshemaraja, *Shiva Sutra Vimarshini,* II.6.
3. See Patanjali, *Yoga Sutras,* I.26: *Sa esha pūrveshāmapi guruh kālena anavecchedāt*—"God is the Guru of even the most ancient Gurus."
4. See *Yoga Vasishtha,* "Nirvana Prakarana," 28.6: *Darshanāt sparshanāt shabdāt kripayā shishya dehake, / Janayedyaha samāvesham shāmbhavam sahi deshika*—"Only one who can give a disciple the auspicious experience of his grace through a look or touch or word is called the Guru." Also see *Kularnava Tantra,* XII.104: *Guravo bahava santi dīpavachcha gruhe gruhe, / Durlabho'yam gurur devi sūryavat sarvadīpakaha*—"Every house has a lamp, and in the same way there are many Gurus, but rare is the Guru, who, like the sun, gives light to all."
5. See *Kularnava Tantra,* XIII: *Guror yasyaiva samsparshāt parānando'bhi jayate*—"He is a Guru through whose touch a disciple experiences the supreme bliss."
6. See *Malini Vijaya Tantra,* 11.10, in which Shiva says, *Sa guror matsamaha prokto mantravīrya prakāshakaha*—"That Guru who reveals the potency of the mantra is just like Me."
7. See *Guru Gita,* v. 46: *Gukārastvandhakārashcha rukāresteja uchyate.*
8. *See Kularnava Tantra,* XII.85: *Guravo bahavahsanti shishya vittāpahārakāhā/durlabho'yam gururdevi shishya duhkāpahārakaha*—"There are many Gurus who steal their disciples' money but very few who steal their pain and suffering."
9. See Narada, *Bhakti Sutras,* v. 5: *Yat prāpya na kinchit vānchati na shochati na/ dveshti na ramate not sahi bhavati*—"After attaining the inner love, a person has no desire for anything else."

THE RELIGION OF THE SELF

Why do you look for Him
  only in churches or mosques?
Do you not see His creation?
Where does He not abide?
The whole universe made by Him
  recites His tale.

— Sarmad

The God Who Dwells in All

Everyone should learn how to welcome others with love and respect. This is true worship and true religion. If a religion does not teach love, respect, and regard for others, it cannot be the religion of humanity.

Once the great being Abu ben Adam was meditating, when his room was suddenly filled with light. From the light emerged a heavenly nymph holding a book with a golden cover. She opened the book and said to Adam, "In this book I am writing the names of all those who follow the highest religion."

"I haven't been following any particular religion," Adam said. "All that I do is meditate with the awareness that everything is the Self. When I look at my neighbors, I consider them to be flames of the one divine being, and I think of myself in the same way."

The nymph vanished. The next day while Adam was meditating, she appeared in the same light. She showed the book to him again, and he saw that his was the only name that had been recorded.

Abu ben Adam had the correct understanding about religion. The Upanishads say that there is one God for everyone in this world. It is not that God lives in the seventh heaven or that He dwells only in a temple, in a mosque, or in a place where bigots who have forgotten the true essence of religion follow the teaching of one sect or another. God is one for all. He lives in all groups, in all temples, in all mosques, and in all churches. Although He is everywhere, He dwells specifically in the human heart. The heart is the divine temple of God.

There are many religions, and each one is fine in its own right. But how many Gods are there to bestow their grace on the followers of all these religions? Is God Hindu? Is He Christian? Is He Jewish? Is He Muslim? Is He Buddhist? Is He black? Is He white? Is He red? To whom does God belong? People address Him in many different ways. Hindus call Him Rama and Christians call Him God. For Muslims He is Allah, and for Zoroastrians He is Zarathustra. But although He has many names, He is one. Therefore, we should learn how to cultivate the awareness of universal brotherhood. We should not pursue religions in order to murder one another with distinctions. All countries, all languages, all races, and all religions belong to Him. He exists in all religions, but He did not create them. If He had, we could not call Him God; we would have to call Him a politician. Why would God create so many religions and make people fight with one another? It is we who have drawn religious boundaries.

The great Sufi saint Jalal-ud-Din Rumi had four disciples who came from four different countries. Once he told them a story. A Persian, a Turk, a Greek, and an Arab were on a pilgrimage. Someone gave them five *rupees* and told them to buy themselves some breakfast. The Persian said, "I'll buy *angur* with this money and we can all eat some." The Turk said, "No, I like *uzum.*" The Greek said, "I don't want to buy anything but *stafyllia.*" The Arab said, "I want to buy *inab!*" The four travelers began to quarrel. Finally, a wise person walked by and asked why they were fighting. After they had told him their story, the wise man said, "Give me your money, and I will buy you all of those things." He went to the market and brought back some grapes. "My *angur*!" said the Persian. "My *uzum*!" said the Turk. "My *stafyllia*!" said the Greek. "My *inab*!" said the Arab. These men had been fighting over a difference in language.

Most religious people are fighting over the same thing. So instead of having blind faith in only one religion, we should have the understanding that God is the same in all religions. What you call water, we call *pani* in Hindi, yet it is only one substance. In the same way, there is only one Truth. Swami Ramakrishna followed every religious path, and they all led him to the same God. For a while he followed Sufism and made the light of Allah reveal itself within him. Then he followed Christianity and saw the divinity of Jesus in his own heart. He worshipped Krishna, and in Krishna he found the same Truth. He was a true knower of religion, and therefore he understood that religion itself is not God, but only points to God. In Hindi, the word "religion" literally means road or path. There are many roads, and they are all good. But the roads end when the temple appears; they no longer have any importance. If we spend all our time fighting over the roads, we will never reach the temple. In the true abode of God, only God exists, and He is completely pure and formless. People who believe in Rama can enter that realm only after they give up their feeling of belonging to Rama. People who believe in Krishna or Jesus can enter it only after they give up their feeling of belonging to Krishna or Jesus. No caste, religion, tradition, or sect can reach that place of God. Once a human being reaches it, he is like a river merging in the ocean. He becomes one with the all-pervasive Absolute.

Because of our ignorance and wrong understanding, we have forgotten our true Self and have become individuals. We have come to believe that we are a certain color and that we are members of a certain class. Similarly, we have come to think that we belong to a certain religion. In worldly life we say, "This is my wife or husband. These are my children. This is my house. These are my cats." In the same way, we say, "This is my religion." Then we become bound by the customs of that religion, and we think, "I cannot go here. I cannot eat that." If we do not have true understanding about religion, we end up blindly following one religion and feeling enmity toward all others. Instead of using our religion to foster love and affection for one another, we use it to encourage hostility and malice and to maintain ideas of differences.

But the truth is that if we belong to God's religion, there is nothing for us to accept or reject, because God's religion is everyone's religion. Once King Akbar asked his prime minister Birbal, "Who is greater, me or God?"

Birbal was very clever. Without hesitation, he answered, "You are, Your Majesty."

Though the king was flattered, he asked, "How can that be?"

"O Your Majesty, if you do not wish to accept someone, you can banish him from your kingdom very easily. But how can God banish anyone from His kingdom? Where can He send him?"

Most religious people are like Akbar; they accept only those who belong to their religion and banish everyone else. But if a religion excludes anyone, then it is not the religion of God. God is all-pervasive, so whom can God reject?

I do not belong to any religion. God accepts everyone, and every religion belongs to Him, so I also accept all religions and all people. Because I am a worshipper of God, I am a worshipper of humanity. If there is no humanity, then there is no God. Before I start my lectures, I always bow my head before everyone and say, "I welcome you all with all my heart with great respect and love." I do this not to please people or to flatter them, but with the awareness that God dwells in every human being. I have complete confidence in this not because I have blind faith, but because it is my direct experience. After meditating for a long time and putting forth a great deal of effort, I experienced Him within me through the grace of my Guru. You too, when you attain God, will discover Him in your heart. Once you perceive Him within, you will also see Him in everyone else, and then you will understand why the true religion is to welcome another human being.

Sons of God

Q: Christianity teaches that no one can attain God except through His son, Jesus Christ. How can Christians deal with the idea that there are many paths to the Truth? This is a source of great inner conflict to me.

SM: If you were to look upon everyone who has seen the Truth as a son of God, then you would not feel this way. In the *Bhagavad Gita,* the Lord says that He manifests Himself from time to time to uplift humanity.[1] So there is no need for conflict. Let your heart be filled with love for God and be grateful to whoever teaches the truth of God. In this way, you will certainly find Him.

I have no doubt that God walks on all paths and has had many sons. Besides Jesus, many saints from all traditions have become one with God. Such Sufis as Shems Tabriez and Mansur Mastana and such Hindus as Tukaram and Jnaneshwar attained the Supreme. God's court is open to everyone.

Many religious groups claim that theirs is the only path to the Truth. The Hare Krishna people claim that one cannot be redeemed unless one believes in Krishna. Muslims claim that one cannot be redeemed unless one has faith in the Koran. Christians claim that one cannot be redeemed unless one follows Christ. The followers of other religions make similar statements. But God never made an agreement with any of these religions. All religions are of fairly recent origin, but God has existed since the beginning of time. He could not have signed a contract with any religious founder saying, "You are my exclusive salesman." The significance of a religion is its emphasis on turning within, not its confidence in its assumed superiority over other religions.

Why Religion Has Not Changed the World

Q: Your message is not new. Other teachers, such as Moses and Jesus, said the same things, yet it seems to me that the world has not changed much. Is there something about people that makes them fail to understand the messages that are given to them?

SM: Most of the people who tell others to follow a religion do not practice religion themselves. Instead, they create fights in the name of religion. I have never heard that Jesus told his followers to hate people of other religions. Nor have I ever heard that Moses told Jews not to look well upon others. Jesus said, "The kingdom of God lies within." When Moses asked God what he should tell people about Him, God said, "Tell them I am that I am." But who has learned these teachings? If a Jew has learned the teaching "I am that I am," then he is a true Jew. If a Christian has come to understand the statement "The kingdom of God is within," then there is no room for conflict. If a Hindu has become aware of the truth of "I am That," then there is no reason for him to fight with others. Only when people forget the understanding of equality do they develop attachment and repulsion. People should follow the religion of oneness, and then they will act with love toward everyone. That is the kind of religion the world needs.

Prayer and Meditation

Q: What is the difference between prayer and meditation?
SM: The final stage of prayer is meditation. When you pray and pray to God, you finally become completely absorbed in Him. That is called meditation.

The Delusion of Theology

There was a great seeker in Delhi named Bullah Shah. For forty years he studied many religions and philosophies and took initiation from every teacher he came across. Yet he did not make any progress. The only things he attained were a mind filled with doubts and a head burdened with the knowledge he had received from so many scriptures and teachers. Finally, his head became so heavy with knowledge that he could not hold it straight. One day a friend asked him what was wrong.

"O friend," said Bullah Shah, "how can I describe my condition to you? I am carrying around so much weight and I cannot get rid of it."

The friend said, "I know someone who can help you," and he took Bullah Shah to the great Siddha, Inayat Shah.

"O sir," said the friend, "here is a man who has studied all the philosophies and is carrying an enormous weight of learning in his head. If you could help him to discard some of it, he would be very grateful to you."

"All right," the master said to Bullah Shah. "Leave your bundle of books somewhere else, and spend some time with me." So Bullah Shah stayed with the great Siddha, and after a few days, Inayat Shah touched him and whispered something in his ear. In that instant, all the weight that Bullah Shah had been carrying was lifted. Bullah Shah was a very ripe seeker, so his awareness immediately turned within, and he began to dwell in the inner Self.

When he returned home, he threw away all his books and began to tell everyone he met that peace and bliss lie within, not in books, temples, or mosques. "You cannot find God in scriptures or in holy places," he would say. "Do not bother with those things. Just turn within, and you will find God."

When the orthodox teachers heard what Bullah Shah was saying, they all turned against him. They called a great assembly and summoned him to come before it.

"Bullah Shah," they said, "you have been speaking against religion. You have committed a great sin."

"If I have committed a sin, then surely I should be feeling pain," said Bullah Shah. "But instead of pain, I am feeling joy, and all my agony has left me. If I have committed a sin, what punishment have you prescribed for me?"

"For your heresy, we are going to brand your body with a red-hot iron bar," said the priests. "There is no sin worse than heresy."

"I will accept this punishment, but first let me ask you something. Suppose that a religious teacher told an innocent person that if he followed a certain practice, he might attain something tomorrow, or in one year, or in ten years, and in this way forty years went by and the poor seeker did not attain anything from the teacher. What punishment would you prescribe for such a teacher?"

"That would be a horrible sin!" they said. "If someone who has nothing to give makes others work for nothing, his body should be branded in twenty places."

"Do you all agree with that?" asked Bullah Shah.

"Yes, we do," said the priests.

"All of you deceived me for forty years. You made me study various scriptures and you forced me to practice techniques and rituals, yet I did not receive anything. So all of your bodies should be branded instead of mine!"

The Men Who Drew Circles

Once a yogi, a priest, and Sheikh Nasrudin were talking about God. At one point they asked each other, "What do you offer to God every month?"

The yogi drew a circle on the ground and said, "Everything I get I throw into the air. Whatever falls inside the circle is for God, and whatever falls outside the circle is for me."

The priest also drew a circle. "Everything I get," he said, "I throw into the air. Whatever falls inside the circle is for me, and whatever falls outside the circle is for God."

Nasrudin said, "Well, I don't do either of those things. I throw everything into the air and say, 'O God, accept whatever You want!' Then whatever falls on the ground is for me."

Many religious people are like Nasrudin. They think that they are giving everything to God, but they are really keeping it all for themselves.

Incarnation of God

Q: Was Christ God-incarnate? What is the difference between you and Christ?

SM: Christ was God-incarnate, Mohammed was God-incarnate, Buddha was God-incarnate, and you and I are God-incarnate. Whoever manifested from the Truth is God-incarnate. We all came out of the same light. Jesus was God-incarnate in a special way, because he had realized his oneness with God. All the great beings shared this characteristic. Nonetheless, everyone is born from God; everyone is an incarnation of God.

No More Roles to Play

Q: What is our role in the cosmos? In what way are we useful to God?

SM: It is not a question of being useful to God. When a person turns within and realizes his own Self, he becomes God. Once he attains Self-realization, the only role that is left for him is to engage himself in God's work, to remain in the wisdom of God and teach others about Him, and to bring the souls that are separated from God back to Him.

God as He Is

Q: Do you consider God to be a personal deity or higher consciousness?

SM: I worship God exactly as He is, without any conditions. It does not matter how you worship God, as long as you do it with love. Once a very religious priest was traveling somewhere by sea, and in the course of his journey he landed on an island. There he came across three very simple beings who were bowing to the rocks, the trees, and the water and praying, "O Lord, You have become all these things. Please accept our prayer."

When the priest heard them, he was shocked. "You haven't learned to pray correctly," he said. "What is the point of bowing to water, to trees, and to rocks?"

The men begged the priest's forgiveness. "No one has ever come to teach us," they said. "Please be our Guru."

The priest taught them the art of praying, and then he went back to his boat and set sail. A little while later, he saw the three men rushing toward him on the water. When they reached the ship, they cried, "O priest, we forgot how to pray as you taught us; we forgot how to pray properly. Please give us another lesson."

The priest was flabbergasted. "How did you manage to walk on the water?"

"Before starting out," the men said, "we prayed, 'O God, You are so powerful! Please thicken the water so that we can walk on it!' And the water became thicker."

When the priest saw the results of their simple devotion, his pretension left him. "It is you who know the true meaning of prayer," he said. "Please teach me."

To reach God, you simply have to pray to Him with love and faith, to worship Him as He is, without trying to impose conditions on Him.

The Means of Attaining Him

God does not want people to sacrifice their lives to Him. He only wants everyone to experience love. He only desires everyone's benefit, because He loves happiness. God's teachings are very pure and sacred. He gives them to the founders of religions and then sends them into the world. Because God Himself is the embodiment of divinity, He inspires everyone to attain the Self. God is the light of peace and justice. Purity and equality are His nature. Love and devotion are the means of attaining Him.

The True Religion

Once a rich man decided to build a temple to Vishnu, so that devotees of Vishnu could worship their deity. But to his chagrin he found that only a few worshippers of Vishnu were visiting the temple. At last he decided to replace the image of Vishnu with one of Rama. Now the worshippers of Vishnu stopped coming, and some devotees of Rama began to visit, but very few ever came. The man said, "Rama isn't attracting anyone either," and he changed the idol to Shiva. Now the worshippers of both Vishnu and Rama stopped coming, and devotees of Shiva started coming, though again there were very few. The man said, "Everybody must be worshipping Shakti, the Divine Mother. I'll be able to draw people by making a new temple to Her." But when he did this, all the worshippers of Vishnu, Rama, and Shiva stopped coming, and just a few worshippers of the Goddess visited the temple. The man thought, "Hinduism simply does not attract people." So he demolished the temple and built a mosque, and then the

Hindus stopped coming and one or two Muslims came. This did not satisfy the man either, so he tore down the mosque and built a church, and now the Muslims stopped coming and the church drew just a few Christians. Finally, the man decided that he would have nothing to do with any house of worship. Instead, he built a tennis court and a health club. Then many people from all sects and religions—worshippers of Rama, Shiva, Vishnu, the Divine Mother, Allah, and Christ—began to come.

This is the problem with religions and sects. None of them works for everyone. An outer religion cannot be equally natural to all, because it is something that is acquired. Only the religion of the Self is natural to everyone, because the Self has been with everyone from time immemorial. The Self within is our own; it cannot be alien to us. If we follow the religion of our own Self, we will be free of fear. To have faith in the Self within is the highest understanding and the true essence of all religions.

In the *Bhagavad Gita,* Krishna expounds the religion of the Self to Arjuna. He says that it is the sovereign knowledge and the sovereign secret, which is supremely purifying, which can be known by direct experience, and which is very easy to practice.[2] What is this knowledge? Krishna explains, *Mayā tatamidam sarvam jagadavyaktamūrtinā; /matshāni sarva bhūtāni nachāham teshvavasthitah*[3]—"All this universe is pervaded by Me, through My unmanifest form. All beings dwell in Me." Whatever we see in this universe, whether animate or inanimate, whether mobile or immobile, has emanated from God and lives in Him. Whether God is giving birth to the world through His divine energy or gathering it back into His being, He does it for no purpose other than His own play, His joyful unfolding. To understand this is true knowledge.

Once I was given a tour of an atomic energy station. The first thing I saw was an enormous pile of metal, rocks, and other materials. Everything in the pile was crushed into a fine powder, which was transferred to a large tank full of boiling water. The powder gradually dissolved, emitting a mild bluish glow. At the next stage, the fluid separated into two parts. One consisted of rays of light, and the other was transformed again into tiny particles of matter. The particles were collected into a small, dense sphere. The scientists there explained to me that all the material in the sphere was nothing but energy. "In fact," they said, "whatever you see is nothing but energy. You may see trees, but they are really energy; you may see water, but that is really energy. Everything you see is nothing but a constant flow of energy."

"This is wonderful," I said, "because our scriptures also say that everything is a form of the same energy, and now you have demonstrated it scientifically."

To have the awareness that everything is made of one conscious energy is not only the highest science but the highest religion. No matter what we accomplish in the world, if we do not achieve this awareness of equality, none of it will be of any use. The *Bhagavad Gita* says, *Samatvam yoga uchyate*[4]—"Yoga is equality-awareness." One who meditates, even for an instant, with the awareness that all objects are a creation of the same God, a reflection of the same divine glory, is following the highest religion.

The great Sufi saint Shems Tabriez said, "Do not think that God is only in your heart. You should be able to recognize Him in every garden, in every forest, in every house, and in every person. You should be able to see Him in your destination, in all the stages of your journey, and in all your fellow pilgrims. You should be able to see Him on every path, in every philosophy, and in every group. You should be able to see Him in all acts, in all deeds, in all thoughts and feelings, and in all expressions of them. You should be able to recognize Him not only in inner lights, but also in the lights that you see in the outer world. All colors and even the darkness are the same Being. If you really love Him, if you want to find His love and be blessed by it, then see Him in every corner of the universe."

This is the true religion. This is the religion of the Self. And this is the religion that will lead us to the goal of all religions.

Notes

1. See *Bhagavad Gita,* IV.7: *Yadā yadā hi dharmasya glānir bhavati bhārata; /abhyutthanam adharmasya tadātmānam srijāmyaham*—"Whenever there is a decline of righteousness, O Arjuna, and a rise of unrighteousness, then I manifest Myself"; IV.8: *Parit rānāya sādhunām vināsāya cha dushkritām; dharmasamsthāpanārthāya sambhavāmi yuge yuge*—"For the protection of the good, for the destruction of the wicked, and for the establishment of righteousness, I am born in every age."
2. Ibid., IX.2: *Rajavidyā rajāguhyam pavitramidamuttamam; /pratyakshāvagamam dharmyam susukham kartumavyayam*—"This is the sovereign science, the sovereign secret, the supreme purifier, realizable by direct intuitional knowledge, according to righteousness, very easy to perform, and imperishable."
3. Ibid., IX.4.
4. Ibid., II.48.

EPILOGUE

Do not hate or hurt anyone.
Make friends with everyone,
For your own Self exists
in every face.
Enjoy the sport of love.
The earth, the sky, the universe
are all the form of the Lord,
the abode of joy.
God permeates every particle of your being.

— Kabir

Life Is a Play of Sun and Shadow

If you were to examine your life with an outlook filled with the knowledge of humanity, you would realize that it is nothing but a play of sunlight and shadow, that it is not different from a drama, or from a joyful dream. This play of creation is filled with unique colors and manifestations. Like clouds in the autumn sky which keep forming and dissolving, forming and dissolving, in your life different colors shine and sparkle for a while and then fade away. You never know why they come and go, or for how long they have been arising and subsiding.

You divide your life into the waking and dream states, but it is all one state. It is ever-new, neither true nor false. What was real yesterday is unreal today, and what is real now will be unreal tomorrow, because tomorrow it will no longer exist. Life is the extraordinary play of the actor of the universe,[1] the Self. It is a mystery, a story told by a grandmother, real, yet without foundation. In this world, day becomes night and night becomes day. Joy turns into grief and grief into joy. Virtue turns into sin and sin into virtue. Birth becomes death and death becomes birth. Success becomes failure and failure becomes success. One person's victory is another's defeat. One person's interest is another's indifference. One person's religion is another's irreligion. The world constantly changes.

This life unfolds from a formless source. It arises from the ocean of bliss, from the joyous swaying of love, and merges back into the space of Consciousness. When he understands the way of the world, the sport and play of destiny, the continuity of the waking and dream states, and the light of the knowledge of Bhairava,* a wise person becomes filled with the extraordinary mystery of the formless and feels lighthearted with this simple awareness. Then he naturally takes delight in the game; with great bliss he swims in the sweet current of love. He lives in a natural way. His is a perfect life in which there is no basis for worry, no reason to be grave, no desire for a support, no binding limitation, no friend to be attached to, no foe to hate. All that remains for him everywhere is the infinite flame of the Self. In him the knowledge of the play of *maya* and the understanding of the great Bhairava are born.

Everything emerges from Bhairava, the conscious Self. To know this is to attain the ever-scintillating knowledge of Bhairava. When you recognize the Self within, an inner smile blossoms, and the peacock of your mind dances in the fountain of the love of life. You realize that life depends on love, and the strings of the *veena* of your heart are strummed. Then you make your life's journey very easily and with great joy, as a guest, as a sightseer, as a witness. For you there is no burden, there is no weeping, there is no boredom. Instead, you sing and dance. Lightheartedly, with great simplicity, you find Consciousness, the center of the universe, within you. This untouched Consciousness is the formless witness, the indestructible joy. It is a drop of nectar; it is the inner heart; it is the shimmering, clear, and beautiful blue light; it is the bliss of the Self which arises independently within; it is the inner pulsation.

Which path will lead you to that state? From what viewpoint can you see it? Look at your life. Look at the inner effulgence. Watch the colors as they arise and disperse. Watch the clouds which come and go in the space of your mind. Look at the space between two thoughts. Look at the patterns of sun and shadow which form and dissolve. See everything as a vast picture composed of countless vessels filled with strange

---

*A name for the supreme reality.

and colorful things, each more fascinating and astounding than the last.

What is all this? It is nothing but the dance of your own Self, the supreme actor. Everything has come from Him. All faces are His. All names are His. All attributes are His. A woman belongs to Him and a man belongs to Him. Attachment and aversion, good and evil, grief and joy, religion and irreligion all belong to Him. Everything arises from Him, and it is all the play of the Self.

What will you attain in this manifold and unique play? You will attain your own nature, your own face. You will perceive the drama of your own life as if it were someone else's life. You will perceive the conscious Self. In your present state, you get angry, you laugh, you weep, you become disappointed. Sometimes you are depressed and sometimes you are elated, and in this way you flow in the current of life. But when you understand that this entire play is a dream, when you attain knowledge, all these things will depart. What else will leave you? Your mask, your facade, your dry and joyless smile, your pride and honor, your pretension and ego, your bigotry, and your wrong understanding's claim to be the Truth—all these things will go. The knot of the heart which makes you imagine that Consciousness is matter will be released. The veil of ignorance which forms a wall between you and God will be rent. You will glimpse the light of the knowledge of Bhairava within. Then you will experience the lightheartedness of Consciousness, the thought-free state, and the independent freshness of the Self, which does not come from eating or drinking, giving or taking. You will experience immeasurable ecstasy, continual inner joy. The tender, sweet, enchanting notes of the divine flute will sound from within.

As the inner wisdom of Bhairava arises, a center of Consciousness, a witness, will form inside you, watching everything but remaining apart from it. You will experience that conscious witness in your heart, the dwelling place of joy and of the divine miracles of the Self. The knowledge of the Self will arise, revealing unique manifestations and infinite colors. You have been searching for this inner light of Consciousness, and when you obtain it you will become free from all imaginary clouds, from the illusory patterns of sun and shadow. In everything, in all forms, you will see only different expressions of your own face. You will come to know that everything is the play of your own mind. No matter where you look you will see that play. The knowledge "I am everything" will arise, and you will see the same Self shining within you and within everyone. The inner knower will come to recognize that he is being reflected everywhere and that it is his own reflection which is constantly passing before him. Wherever you look you will see your own Self. Then you will begin to wonder, "Do I exist in the world or does the world exist in me?"

One who has experienced his own Self has solved the mystery of the game of life. Behind everything there is great love. There is Consciousness. There is the Guru's compassion. There is the extraordinary, yet subtle desire to be reunited with the Self. When you attain the knowledge of Bhairava, you will be reunited with the Self. You will be awakened within.

Can you be awakened? Can you drink the nectar of your own love? With the knowledge of That, can you laugh joyfully day and night within yourself? Can you recognize your own Self in countless forms? If you can do so, your life will be truly alive. Then through the inner understanding, through the light of Chit Kundalini, through the knowledge of Bhairava, the seed of the movement of the Self will sprout. You will see your own Self in everyone. You will attain what you have already attained. You will find what you have never lost.

In you, of you, and for you,

Your own,

स्वामी मुक्तानंद.

Swami Muktananda

Note

1. See *Shiva Sutras,* III.9: *Nartaka ātmā*—"The Self is the actor."

SWAMI MUKTANANDA'S ASHRAM, GURUDEV SIDDHA PEETH, IN GANESHPURI, INDIA

GLOSSARY

Aham brahmasmi: One of the four *mahavakyas,* or great statements, of Vedanta. It means "I am Brahman," the supreme Absolute.

Allah: Name of God in the Muslim religion.

Arjuna: Famous warrior and one of the heroes of the *Mahabharata* epic. It was to Arjuna that Krishna imparted the teaching of the *Bhagavad Gita.*

Asana: 1. Hatha yoga posture practiced to strengthen the body, purify the nerves, and develop one-pointedness of mind; the yoga texts refer to eighty-four *asanas.* 2. Seat or mat on which one sits for meditation.

Ashram: Institution or community where spiritual discipline is practiced; abode of a saint or holy man.

Ashtavakra: Famous sage in the Indian epics and the Puranas whose body was deformed in eight places. His teachings are contained in the *Ashtavakra Gita.*

Austerity: 1. Difficult spiritual practice. 2. Abandonment of worldly pleasures for the purpose of spiritual attainment.

Bartruhari: A king who renounced his kingdom in order to become a yogi; author of many moral and spiritual poems.

Bhagavad Gita: One of the great works of spiritual literature in which Lord Krishna explains the path of liberation to Arjuna on the battlefield during the war described in the *Mahabharata.*

Bhairava: A name of Shiva, the supreme reality.

Brahma: One of the trinity of Hindu deities; creator of the universe.

Brahmadeva: See Brahma.

Brahman: Vedantic term for the absolute reality.

Chiti: Divine conscious energy; creative aspect of the Absolute.

Consciousness: The intelligent, supremely autonomous energy that pervades and supports everything in the cosmos. See Chiti.

Dho'l-Nun: Ninth century Sufi saint.

Ego: Limited "I"-awareness, which identifies with limiting attributes such as the mind or the body.

Ekanath Maharaj (1528 – 1609): Householder poet-saint of Maharashtra reknowned for his scriptural commentaries and spiritual poetry.

Five elements: Ether, fire, air, water, earth.

Gauranga (also known as Chaitanya Mahaprabhu): Original Guru of the Hare Krishna movement, who stressed chanting as the means of attaining God.

Guru: Spiritual master who has attained oneness with God and who initiates others into the spiritual path and guides them to liberation.

Hanuman: Devotee and servant of Rama. His form was that of a monkey of great strength.

Hatha yoga: Yogic discipline through which the *samadhi* state is attained by union of the *prana* and *apana,* the incoming and outgoing breaths. Various bodily and mental exercises are practiced to purify the nervous system and bring about the even flow of *prana.*

Hazrat Basjid Bastami:Ninth century Sufi saint of Baghdad; author of numerous poems describing the state of union with God.

Homeopathy: System of medicine that treats diseases by the administration of minute doses of a remedy that would in a healthy person produce symptoms of the disease.

Hubli: Small town in the Karnataka state of India; home of Siddharudha Swami.

Jamuna River: Holy river in north India on the banks of which Lord Krishna spent his youth.

Janaka: Saintly king of Mithila in ancient India; father of Sita, Lord Rama's consort.

Japa: Repetition of mantra.

Jnaneshwar Maharaj (1275 – 1296): Highly revered poet-saint of Maharashtra. His verse commentary on the *Bhagavad Gita — Jnaneshwari*—written in the Marathi language, is acknowledged as one of the world's most important spiritual works.

Kabir (1440– 1518): Renowned Indian poet-saint who was a weaver in Benares. His followers were both Hindus and Muslims, and his influence was a powerful force in overcoming religious factionalism.

Karma: Physical, mental, or verbal action or the results of such action.

Kashmir Shaivism: Nondual philosophy that recognizes the entire universe as a manifestation of Chiti, the divine conscious energy.

Koran: Major sacred text of the Muslim religion.

Krishna: Eighth incarnation of Vishnu, whose life story is described in the *Shrimad Bhagavatam* and the *Mahabharata* and whose teachings are contained in the *Bhagavad Gita.*

Kularnava Tantra: Treatise on the practice of yoga; basic work of the Kaula school of tantrism.

Mansur Mastana: Ecstatic tenth century Sufi saint who proclaimed, *Anal-haq* ("I am the Absolute") and was hanged by the government of the Caliph in Baghdad.

Mantra: Sacred word or sound invested with the power to transform or protect one who repeats it.

Maya: Force that shows the unreal as real and presents that which is temporary and short-lived as permanent and everlasting.

Organs of action: Powers that control the actions of speech, grasping, locomotion, procreation, and excretion.

Prasad: 1. A blessed or divine gift. 2. Food that has been blessed by being offered to God.

Rajasthan: State in mid-central India.

Ramakrishna Paramahamsa (1836 – 1886): The most famous of modern Indian saints; Guru of Vivekananda and the founder of the Ramakrishna Order.

Rumi, Jalal-ud-Din: Thirteenth century Sufi poet-saint.

Sadhana: Practice of spiritual discipline.

Sadhu: Holy being.

Samadhi: State of meditative union with the Absolute.

Sannyasa: Initiation into monkhood in the Indian tradition.

Sannyasi: Monk in the Indian tradition.

Sanskrit: The most ancient of languages. Most of the classical spiritual texts of India are written in Sanskrit.

Senses of perception: Hearing, seeing, touching, tasting, smelling.

Shankaracharya (788–820): One of the major philosopher-saints of the Indian tradition, who expounded the philosophy of absolute nondualism (Advaita).

Shems Tabriez: Tenth century Sufi saint.

Shiva: 1. Name for the all-pervasive supreme reality. 2. One of the trinity of Hindu deities. He is known as the supreme Guru, and many of the important texts of Kashmir Shaivite philosophy are in the form of dialogues between Shiva and his consort Parvati.

Shiva Purana: One of the eighteen Puranas, or sacred books, containing stories, legends, and hymns about the creation of the universe, the incarnations of God, and the spiritual legacies of great sages and kings.

Shiva Sutras: Sanskrit text which Shiva revealed to the sage Vasuguptacharya.

Shukạ: One of the legendary Puranic sages of ancient times.

Siddha: Perfected yogi.

Siddharudha Swami: Twentieth century saint and expounder of Vedanta in whose ashram at Hubli Swami Muktananda studied as a young monk.

Sufi: Practitioner of Sufism.

Sufism: Mystical tradition related to the Muslim religion which teaches that the goal of life is realization of the divine principle in the heart.

Suki: Village in Maharashtra.

Sunderdas (1596 – 1689): Renowned Indian poet-saint born in Rajasthan.

Swami: Title given to an Indian monk.

Tukaram Maharaj (1608–1650): Revered and popular poet-saint of Maharashtra and author of thousands of devotional songs.

Tulasidas (1532–1623): North Indian poet-saint and author of the Tulasi *Ramayana.*

Upanishads: Teachings of the ancient sages on the essential nature of existence. They comprise the end portion of the Vedas.

Vasishtha: Ancient sage and Guru of Lord Rama. The *Yoga Vasishtha,* one of the most important Indian scriptural works, consists of his teachings to Lord Rama.

Vedanta: Philosophical school founded by Badarayana containing the teachings of the Upanishads and investigating the nature of the relationship between the Absolute, the world, and the Self.

Veena: Indian stringed instrument.

Vijnana Bhairava: Important text of Kashmir Shaivism containing 112 *dharanas,* or centering techniques, through which the Absolute is realized.

Vishnu: One of the trinity of Hindu deities; God as the preserver.

Vivekananda, Swami (1863 – 1902): Disciple of Ramakrishna Paramahamsa and one of the most influential spiritual figures in modern India. During numerous trips to the West, he introduced the teachings of Vedanta to Westerners.

Woodroffe, Sir John: Former Indian Supreme Court justice in Calcutta who became a highly respected scholar in the Indian tantric tradition; author of many books.

Yoga (*lit.* "union"): State of oneness with the Self; the practices leading to that state.

Yoga Sutras: Authoritative text on yoga composed by the sage Patanjali.

Yogi: One who practices yoga; also one who has attained the goal of yoga.

INDEX

OTHER PUBLICATIONS

By Swami Muktananda

The Perfect Relationship The Guru/disciple relationship
Secret of the Siddhas Swami Muktananda on Siddha Yoga and Kashmir Shaivism
Does Death Really Exist? A perspective on death and life
Mystery of the Mind How to deal with the mind
Reflections of the Self Poems of spiritual life
Play of Consciousness Muktananda's spiritual autobiography
Satsang with Baba (Five Volumes) Questions and answers
Muktananda-Selected Essays Edited by Paul Zweig
Meditate Muktananda's basic teaching on meditation
In the Company of a Siddha Muktananda talks with pioneers in science, consciousness and spirituality
Light on the Path Essential aspects of the Siddha path
Siddha Meditation* Commentaries on the Shiva Sutras and other ancient texts
Mukteshwari I & II Poetic aphorisms
I Am That The science of Hamsa mantra
Kundalini: The Secret of Life Muktananda's teachings on our innate spiritual energy
Small books of aphorisms: I Welcome You All With Love, God Is With You, A Book for the Mind, I Love You*, and **To Know the Knower.**

About Swami Muktananda

A Search for the Self by Swami Prajnananda. Swami Muktananda's biography
Muktananda Siddha Guru* by Shankar (Swami Shankarananda). Introduction to Muktananda and his teachings.

Other Books

Introduction to Kashmir Shaivism The philosophy most closely reflecting Muktananda's teaching
Understanding Siddha Yoga, Volumes I & II Textbooks on Siddha Yoga
Nectar of Chanting Sacred chants sung regularly in Muktananda's Ashrams. Sanskrit translation with transliteration
Lalleshwari Poems of a great woman saint
Hatha Yoga for Meditators A detailed guide to Hatha Yoga as taught in Swami Muktananda's Ashrams
Shree Guru Gita Word-by-word translation with transliteration and original Sanskrit

Publications

Gurudev Siddha Peeth Newsletter Monthly from Muktananda's Ashram in India
Shree Gurudev Vani Annual Journal by devotees
Siddha Path Monthly magazine of SYDA Foundation

* **Also available in Braille** Complete with photographs

If you want more information about these books, write to SYDA Bookstore, P.O. Box 605, South Fallsburg, N.Y. 12779.

MAJOR CENTERS AND ASHRAMS

There are over 300 Siddha Yoga Meditation Centers and residential Ashrams around the world. They all hold regular programs which are free and open to the public. Many of them also conduct Siddha Yoga Meditation Intensives and Introductory Programs. Contact any of the following major Centers for the location of the Center nearest you.

UNITED STATES

SYDA Foundation New York
P.O. Box 600
South Fallsburg, New York 12779
Phone: (914)434-2000
(212)247-5997

SYDA Foundation Ann Arbor
1520 Hill
Ann Arbor, Michigan 48104
Phone: (313)994-5625
994-3072

Siddha Yoga Dham Atlanta
1473 Fairview Rd., N.E.
Atlanta, Georgia 30306
Phone: (404)378-7932

SYDA Foundation Boston
Fernwood Road—Manor House
Chestnut Hill, Massachusetts 02167
Phone: (617)734-0137

Siddha Yoga Meditation Ashram Chicago
2100 W. Bradley Place
Chicago, Illinois 60618
Phone: (312)327-0536

Siddha Yoga Dham Cincinnati
157 Ridgeview Drive
Cincinnati, Ohio 45215
Phone: (513) 821-3629

Siddha Yoga Meditation Center Costa Mesa
431 East 20th Street
Costa Mesa, CA 92627
Phone: (714)631-4446

Siddha Yoga Dham Gainesville
1000 SW 9th Street
Gainesville, Florida 32601
Phone: (904)375-7629

Siddha Yoga Dham Hawaii
P.O. Box 10191
Honolulu, Hawaii 96816
3807 Diamond Head Circle
Honolulu, Hawaii 96815
Phone: (808)732-1558

Muktananda Meditation Center Siddha Yoga Dham Houston
3815 Garrott
Houston, Texas 77006
Phone: (713)529-0006

SYDA Foundation Los Angeles
P.O. Box 2157
Santa Monica, California 90406
309 Broadway
Santa Monica, California 90401
Phone: (213)393-1491

SYDA Foundation Manhattan
324 West 86th Street
New York, New York 10024
Phone: (212)873-8030

Siddha Yoga Dham Miami
256 S.W. 12th Street
Miami, Florida 33130
Phone: (305)858-5369

SYDA Foundation Oakland
P.O. Box 11071
Oakland, California 94611
1107 Stanford Avenue
Oakland, California 94608
Phone: (415)655-8677

Siddha Yoga Dham Philadelphia
6429 Wayne Avenue
Philadelphia, Pennsylvania 19119
Phone: (215)849-0888

Siddha Yoga Dham Seattle
1409 N.E. 66th
Seattle, Washington 98115
Phone: (206)523-2583

Siddha Yoga Meditation Center Tucson
2905 N. Camino De Oeste
Tucson, Arizona 85706
Phone: (602)743-7142

Siddha Yoga Dham Washington, D.C.
5015 16th St. N.W.
Washington, D.C. 20011
Phone: (202)882-4377

ARGENTINA

Siddha Yoga Argentina
Calle Hipolito Yrigoyen 3720
Buenos Aires, Argentina
Phone: 782-6246

AUSTRALIA

Siddha Yoga Dham Melbourne
202 Gore Street
Fitzroy, Melbourne VIC 3065
Australia
Phone: (03)419-6299

Siddha Yoga Dham Sydney
1 Warrenball Ave.
Newton NSW 2042, Australia
Phone: (02)519-7540

CANADA

Muktananda Meditation Center Mississauga
6789 Segovia Road, Mississauga
Ontario L5N 1P1, Canada
Phone: (416)826-4512

Centre de Siddha Yoga Montreal
3979 Rue St. Hubert
Montreal, Quebec H2L 4A6
Canada
Phone: (514)524-9020

Muktananda Meditation Society Vancouver
P.O. Box 2990
Vancouver, B.C. V6B 3X4
Canada
Phone: (604)734-7181

ENGLAND

Siddha Yoga Dham London
1 Bonneville Gardens
London SW4 9LB England
Phone: (01)675-4105

FRANCE

Siddha Yoga Dham France
7 Rue du Plaisir
93400 St. Ouen
Paris, France
Phone: (1)258-51-35

GERMANY

Siddha Yoga Dham Germany
Fifchergasse 5
6050 Ossenbach – Main
Federal Republic Germany
Phone: 0611-86 1260

INDIA

Gurudev Siddha Peeth
(WORLD HEADQUARTERS)
P.O. Ganeshpuri (Pin 401 206)
Dist. Thana
Maharashtra, India

Shree Gurudev Ashram New Delhi
Bhatti Village, Mehrauli Block
c/o Khanna, Claridges Hotel
New Delhi South, India 110030

ISRAEL

Siddha Yoga Dham Jerusalem
Harazim St. 10/24 Beit-Hakerem
Jerusalem, Israel
Phone: (02)520184

ITALY

Siddha Yoga Dham Rome
Via Germanico 107
00192 Rome, Italy
Phone: (06)385-063

MEXICO

Siddha Yoga Dham Mexico City
Apartado Postal 41-890
Mexico 10 DF Mexico
Phone: (905)286-1676

NETHERLANDS

Muktananda Siddha Meditation Center Amsterdam
Da Costakade 116 I hoog
1053 XB Amsterdam, Netherlands
Phone: (020)85-1596

NEW ZEALAND

Siddha Yoga Dham Canterbury
351 Gardiners Road
Christchurch 5, New Zealand

PUERTO RICO

Siddha Yoga Dham Puerto Rico
48 M. Rivera Street
Cabo Rojo 00623 Puerto Rico
Phone: (809) 832-7164

SPAIN

Siddha Yoga Dham Barcelona
Alta de San Pedro, 27, 2°
Barcelona, Spain
Phone: (93)325-3197

Siddha Yoga Dham Madrid
Apdo 42 081
Madrid, Spain
Phone: (91)448-8349

SWEDEN

Siddha Yoga Dham Stockholm
Malmgardsv, 59A 11638
Stockholm, Sweden

SWITZERLAND

Muktananda Siddha Meditation Center Bern
Brunngasse 54, 3011
Bern, Switzerland
Phone: (031)22.59.63